LIVES OF GREAT RELIGIOUS BOOKS

The Book of *Genesis*

LIVES OF GREAT RELIGIOUS BOOKS

The Book of *Genesis*

A BIOGRAPHY

Ronald Hendel

PRINCETON UNIVERSITY PRESS

Princeton and Oxford

Copyright © 2013 by Princeton University Press

Published by Princeton University Press, 41 William Street,

Princeton, New Jersey 08540

In the United Kingdom: Princeton University Press, 6 Oxford Street,

Woodstock, Oxfordshire OX20 1TW

press.princeton.edu

Jacket Illustration: *Catholic Church*.[Psalter-Hours of Guiluys de
Boisleux].[Arras, France, 1243 – 1246], MS M.730, fol. 9r. Courtesy of
The Pierpont Morgan Library, New York. MS M.730,fol. 9r. Purchased
from the Holford Estate, 1927.

All Rights Reserved

Library of Congress Cataloging-in-Publication Data

Hendel, Ronald S.

    The book of Genesis : a biography / Ronald Hendel.

        p. cm. — (Lives of great religious books)

    Includes bibliographical references and index.

    ISBN 978-0-691-14012-4 (alk. paper)

    1. Bible. O.T. Genesis—Criticism, interpretation, etc.   I. Title.

    BS1235.52.H46 2013

    222′.1106—dc23   2012015634

British Library Cataloging-in-Publication Data is available

This book has been composed in Garamond Premier Pro

Printed on acid-free paper. ∞

Printed in the United States of America

10 9 8 7 6 5 4 3 2 1

For Bob Alter, friend, colleague,

and fellow Genesiologist

Not to outgrow Genesis, is a sweet monition.

EMILY DICKINSON

CONTENTS

ACKNOWLEDGMENTS

This book owes its birth to many hands. My thanks to Fred Appel for inviting me to contribute a volume to the Lives of Great Religious Books. Since the life of Genesis is so vast, I did what professors do—I designed a course. My thanks to the delightful and inquisitive Berkeley undergraduates who have taken this course ("The Bible in Western Culture"), which is now my favorite offering. Their questions have pushed me to explore things deeply, for which I am grateful. Thanks also to my excellent teaching assistants, Daniel Fisher, Alison Joseph, and Dale Loepp. I relied on many of my faculty colleagues to bring me up to speed on topics ancient, medieval, and modern. Several of them generously commented on drafts of chapters: Steve Justice, Niklaus Largier, Tony Long, Chessie Rochberg, and Jonathan Sheehan. Bob Alter, to whom this book is dedicated, vetted the whole manuscript (and must have noticed his influence in several parts). Yosefa Raz, my research assistant, provided invaluable comments on style and content. With these superb advisors, any flaws in conception and execution are my own stubborn fault. Jodi Beder bravely tamed my prose. Janet

Russell contributed an exemplary index. Bill Propp not only improved my text but, to my delight, conjured seven marvelous illuminations (located at the head of each chapter). Finally, my thanks to Ann, Ed, and Nat, who may actually end up reading this book.

LIVES OF GREAT RELIGIOUS BOOKS

The Book of *Genesis*

The Life of Genesis

Despite predictions of its demise, the book of Genesis is still alive and well in the twenty-first century. From political and religious debates to consumer culture, Genesis is all around us. One has only to glance at the headlines to find controversies that take their heat and light from Genesis. The question of whether the contents of Genesis 1 should be taught in science classes—under the names "creationism" or "intelligent design"—preoccupies school boards and political candidates. Proponents and opponents of gay marriage and gay clergy appeal to the testimony of Genesis. The "new atheist" writers criticize the irrationality of Genesis, much as the old atheists, like Thomas Paine, did more than two centuries ago. Evangelical scholars argue whether Adam and Eve were historical figures.

In our popular and commercial culture, references to Genesis pop up regularly. "Jacobs Ladder" is an upscale exercise machine, priced around $3,000. "Am I My Brother's Keeper" is the name of an album by the hip-hop group Kane and Abel. The Methuselah Foundation supports scientific research into extending human life. Adam and Eve is the name of a sex toy company. Examples of such creative branding could be multiplied indefinitely. Recently an illustrated version of Genesis, by the comics icon R. Crumb, topped the New York Times best-seller list. A favorite tourist destination, the Creation Museum (built in Kentucky by a group called Answers in Genesis), has attracted over a million visitors. This modern shrine to Genesis features high-tech dioramas of the Garden of Eden and Noah's Ark, complete with dinosaurs, a well-muscled Adam, and a supermodel Eve. In its halls Genesis becomes a simulacrum of science, providing comfort for its target audience.

In earlier centuries Genesis was alive in different ways. In the Middle Ages ascetics and mystics tried to gain access to the heavenly Garden of Eden through spiritual exercises. The stories of Genesis were reproduced in illustrations in stained-glass windows and paupers' Bibles. Monks and nuns chanted sublime songs dedicated to the patriarchs. Figs and apples, identified as the forbidden fruit in the Garden of Eden, were eaten as aphrodisiacs. Christians made pilgrimages to great cathedrals and shrines, where they could still perceive the aura of Genesis and its famous events. Although most people could not read the book, the evidence of Genesis was everywhere.

For roughly two and a half thousand years, people in Western culture have been living cheek by jowl with the book of Genesis. It is this mutual engagement—in which Genesis colors our lives, while we strain to understand it—that is the subject of this book. Within the large scope of the life of Genesis, three interwoven themes animate our story: (1) The life of Genesis involves an interplay between its original meanings—its "plain" senses—and its multiple forms of interpretation over the centuries. (2) The life of Genesis involves an ages-long relationship between truth and error, in which the boundaries between the two are fiercely contested. (3) The keys to understanding the book of Genesis in every age correspond to the keys to understanding reality generally. But these keys change over time, and they open different doors. Let us explore these themes and their implications.

Life and Afterlife

A book does not have a life in the most literal sense, because it is not an organic life-form. A book is an object, made of paper—or in the early life of Genesis, papyrus or parchment. We can only say that it has a life in an extended sense, as part of our past and present. The book of Genesis is alive because it is a formative part of the human life-world, and it has been so for a long time. It is the relationship that people have had with this object that gives it a life and makes it a subject for a biography. Its life story—which is what the word "biography" means—is one subplot in the complicated history of our collective life in Western civilization. Its life is a part of our own biography in the long span of human culture.

It is important to make a careful distinction *within* the life of Genesis. This concerns the difference between the book's original meanings—those that are properties of the "plain" or grammatical sense of the ancient Hebrew words, sentences, and narratives—and its later interpretations. The latter often rely on assumptions and categories that are foreign to the world of ancient Israel. For example, interpretations that rely on Platonic philosophy or apocalyptic expectations are anachronistic when applied to Genesis, because these categories of thought were created after the book was written. Like a Shakespeare play set in a rocket ship, this is a transposition of the text into a modern idiom. It is an imaginative revision, which takes liberties with the plain sense, whether self-consciously or not. Later interpretations are usually modernizations of the stories, which keeps their meanings fresh and relevant, but which may diverge significantly from the stories' native conceptual horizons.

Walter Benjamin drew a valuable distinction between a text's "life" and its "afterlife." He wrote, "in its afterlife—which could not be called that if it were not a transformation and a renewal of something living—the original undergoes a change."[1] Through its transformation—or more precisely, its incessant variety of transformations—the text takes on new layers of sense, some of which may have been unthinkable previously. The book becomes a historical agent, which enters into new religious and political configurations. The biography of Genesis includes what Benjamin calls its life *and* its afterlife, its original meanings and its effects on later generations. Its afterlife transforms, renews, and extends its life.

But the life and afterlife of Genesis are not two wholly different things. The plain senses of Genesis are never lost as long as people pay attention to the verbal details and resonances of the text. Even if one believes that the true meaning has to do with abstract spiritual truths or coded prophecies, its narrative force and style are apparent to any careful reader. Its plain meanings are always available, even if they are partially obscured under spiritual castles. As Erich Auerbach observed, it is the narrative style of Genesis—with its mysterious events, laconic dialogue, and sparse background details—that gives rise to the necessity of interpretation: "even the factual and psychological elements ... are mysterious, merely touched upon, fraught with background; and therefore they require subtle investigation and interpretation, they demand them."[2] The life of Genesis, in this respect, demands a rich and complicated afterlife.

A text's afterlife inevitably affects one's reading of it, even if one is trying to attend to its plain or native senses. How difficult is it to read the Garden of Eden story without importing later interpretations, such as Original Sin, Eve as erotic temptress, or the snake as Satan? These are products of Genesis's afterlife, which are hard to see around. The life and afterlife of Genesis are perpetually in a tangled relationship with each other, which is to say that Genesis has a complicated biography.

The Uses of Error

The relationship between the book's life and afterlife raises another complicated issue. One theme within the interpretation of Genesis has been the falsity of many of its interpretations. As we will see, in medieval and early modern times daring commentators such as Rashi and Martin Luther criticized figural interpretations of Genesis as arbitrary or untrue. For Luther, the falsity of much traditional interpretation undermined the authority of the Catholic Church. A century later, Galileo criticized the Church doctrines about biblical cosmology and argued that it was wrong to take the testimony of Genesis as scientific evidence. Half a century later, Spinoza argued that scientific method should be brought to bear on the interpretation of Genesis, casting aside the traditional interpretations of church and synagogue. Modern biblical scholarship also argues that much of the history of the interpretation of Genesis is a history of error.

Why then should we be concerned with the biography of Genesis? If much of its afterlife in Western civilization has been false, or based on faulty premises, why not simply give it an honorable burial? The answer to these questions has to do with the importance of error in human life. As Friedrich Nietzsche compellingly argued, illusion and error are necessary in human life, especially in our collective memory. Too much historical criticism "uproots the future because it destroys illusions and robs existing things of their atmosphere in which alone they can live."[3] People and cultures need illusions in order to live fully, to flourish. If we consider the afterlife of Genesis from this perspective, we can see that it mostly consists of such creative illusions. Sometimes these illusions are profound, providing the means for human life to flourish. Sometimes they are cruel, justifying the forces of injustice and oppression. But in either case, they provide the inevitable atmosphere of human life.

Frank Kermode has commented insightfully about the history of error in biblical interpretation:

> The history of interpretation, the skills by which we keep alive in our minds the light and the dark of past literature and past humanity, is to an incalculable extent a history of error. . . . The history of biblical interpretation will provide many instances of fruitful misunderstanding. It arises because we want to have more of the story than was originally offered, or we want to see into the depths of that story. We have always been pretty sure that the literal sense is not enough, and when we try to go beyond it we may err, but sometimes splendidly.[4]

It is because people want more and more urgent meanings that "fruitful misunderstanding" arises. The stories of Genesis serve as the occasion for such meanings, because Genesis is an authoritative book. That these interpretations are often tissues of error tells us what we already know about humanity—that we are producers and consumers of illusion. (Franz Kafka has a lot to say about this in his reflections on Genesis; see chapter 7.) The afterlife of Genesis is a record of how people have produced, maintained, and repaired this necessary atmosphere over the millennia. There are many uses of error—some beneficial, some reprehensible—but we could hardly survive without them. They are our errors, and we are responsible for them. The biography of Genesis tells us much about the uses of error, both in our lives and the lives of our ancestors.

Genesis and Reality

The interpretation of Genesis in Western civilization opens up another set of issues relating to the question of truth and error. Over the generations, the ways that people have understood Genesis tend to correlate with the ways that people have understood reality. It is not just that Genesis provides an account of the origins of reality—which it does—but that the *kinds* of meaning that people expect to find in Genesis are the same kinds that they expect in the world outside the book. In other words, the ways that people perceive Genesis both shape and reflect their perception of reality. What is perhaps surprising is how radically these ways of perceiving Genesis and reality have changed over time, and how in some respects our perceptions have gone back to the way they were at the time when the book of Genesis was born.

Genesis envisions a single, God-created universe in which human life is limited by the boundaries of knowledge and death. We are earth-bound, intermittently wise, often immoral, mortal creatures. There is often a harsh realism in the Genesis accounts of human life. But in the centuries after the birth of Genesis, two new concepts of reality arose. The first of these was apocalyptic religion, which expects a new era in the future, when the dead will rise and existence will be perfect. In the apocalyptic reinterpretation of Genesis, this will be a return to the Garden of Eden at the End of Days. The second new concept, in origin a Greek import, envisions an invisible "higher" world, which one can attain through wisdom and spiritual discipline. This concept, which was given classic form by Plato, became a dominant concept in Jewish and Christian religious thought. By the third century BCE, most interpretations of Genesis came to be colored by apocalyptic and Platonic views of reality, either separately or mingled together. The interpretation of Genesis in terms of apocalyptic or Platonic meanings is what I call *figural* interpretation. Figural interpretation was the rule for over a thousand years in Judaism and Christianity, until it started to lose its footing in the early modern era, a process that accelerated in the age of science. In the twenty-first century we are still dealing with the problems that accompanied the loss of the figural sense. The meanings of both Genesis and reality have become problematic, and we are still stumbling over how to deal with the loss of the figural sense of things.

The theme of the relationship between realism and figuralism in the life of Genesis derives from the work of Erich Auerbach (whom we will meet in chapter 7). Auerbach showed how the history of Western literature—starting with Genesis and Homer—is also a history of the ways that people have understood reality. This history begins with the different Greek and Hebrew styles of realism. The terse style of Genesis offers a wealth of psychological perspective, a sense of historical becoming, and a concern for the problematic. In contrast, Homer has an elaborately descriptive style in which all things are illuminated, but which gives a static sense of history and character. Western literature begins with these two styles of realism, but in late antiquity and medieval times adopts a figural style, in which texts and reality are figures or prophecies of the World to Come or the Perfect World: "Life on earth is . . . the figure of the life beyond."[5] The figural interpretation of Genesis and reality became problematic in early modern times, and with the Renaissance and the rise of science new forms of realism took root. Western literature therefore began with the realism of Genesis and Greek epic, and returned to a revitalized realism in the modern era.

This trajectory—from realism to figuralism and back again, but at a different level—provides an illuminating story line for the biography of Genesis. A biography can be plotted in innumerable ways, or it can be mostly unstructured, in the manner of Henry Ford's definition of history as "one damn thing after another." My plot will emphasize certain bits of the biography of Genesis and overlook others, but it has the advantage of making a coherent story.

In this plot, the realism of the biblical universe (chapter 1, "The Genesis of Genesis") morphs into a figural dual reality, in which this world is a flawed version of a more perfect world, and Genesis is a cryptic version of a more perfect text (chapter 2, "The Rise of the Figural Sense"). The hidden world, which Genesis reveals, has two modalities: one is in future time, at the End of Days (chapter 3, "Apocalyptic Secrets") and the other is in metaphysical space, the Higher World (chapter 4, "Platonic Worlds"). The kinds of figural worlds that Genesis opens up are not just ideas, but are lived and experienced realities, and have practical and political consequences. People do things with Genesis in order to influence and change reality.

In early modern times (between 1200 and 1600), people in the West began to return to a single world, a universe, in which our lives are bounded spatially by the earth and temporally by death. The foundations of a figural world were undermined (chapter 5, "Between the Figure and the Real"), and so—among other consequences—people began to read Genesis in its plain or realistic sense, not as a cipher about another world. Of course, the real world in Genesis does not precisely map onto the modern scientific view of the world (chapter 6, "Genesis and Science"). Its philosophical concepts don't precisely map onto modern concepts either, yet it remains a part of our moral, religious, and political lives (chapter 7, "Modern Times"). Despite the fact that it is mostly myth and legend, in modern times Genesis is still good to think about and to do things with.

In my view, the modern return to realism is a good thing, because it allows us to read Genesis passionately and critically in the world as it is. Genesis is a magnificent work of religious literature, which still has the capacity to inspire. It represents a world that is real, although its world is created and influenced by miraculous beings (angels, God, and sundry other divine beings). Perhaps we can describe its style as "magical" realism, in the sense that its reality is surrounded and influenced by the supernatural. The category of the magical has become a problem in our modern view of reality, influenced as we are by science and scholarship. We live—or think we live—in a largely disenchanted world. I suggest that our ancient enchantments are still alive in our world, although their forms and influences have changed over time. Religion, art, and culture still draw on the resources of Genesis to explore and articulate reality, even when the veracity of Genesis is contested. To put it in a different way, our pursuit of Genesis and reality still go hand in hand.

But this gets us ahead of our story, which begins with the birth of the book in a small country in the ancient Middle East.

The Genesis of Genesis

CHAPTER 1

"The woman saw that the tree was good for food,
that it was a delight to the eyes, and desirable to
make one wise."

The book of Genesis had a complicated birth, or rather, many births. It is composed of multiple layers of text, composed at different times and with differing interests and emphases. Like the biblical twins Jacob and Esau, who wrestled in their mother's womb, these texts often seem to be rivals. They stake out different claims about the authority of the past and the nature of God and humans. Let us consider what we can plausibly know about the beginnings of Genesis, and then turn to the different Genesis accounts of the beginning.

Old Poetry

The oldest part of Genesis is the tribal poem "The Blessing of Jacob," in Genesis 49. This is the only part of Genesis written in the oldest stratum of Biblical Hebrew.[1] This poem is a collection of tribal blessings and curses. It belongs to the same genre as the blessings and curses in "The Blessing of Moses" in Deuteronomy 33 and "The Song of Deborah" in Judges 5. It is likely that such lists of tribal blessings and curses were recited at tribal gatherings during times of war or during pilgrimage festivals, which were the main occasions when different tribes came together. In Genesis the tribal blessings and curses are spoken by the patriarch Jacob on his deathbed, and they are addressed to his sons, who are the ancestors of the twelve tribes. They are Jacob's prophecy of each tribe's future destiny.

The poem showers praise or blame on each tribe, often focused on the tribe's martial prowess. It does this by making elaborate comparisons with the world of nature. For example, Jacob praises Judah's majestic strength by comparing him with a lion:

A lion's whelp is Judah,
From the prey, O my son, you rise up.
He crouches and lies down like a lion,
And like a young lion, who can rouse him?
(Genesis 49:9)

And Benjamin, the youngest son, is fierce as a wolf:

Benjamin is a ravenous wolf,
In the morning he consumes the spoils,
And in the evening he divides plunder.
(Genesis 49:27)

Notice the muscular animal power in the description of Judah—like a lion he rises up, crouches, and lies down. He is irresistible and immovable. Like the king of beasts, he is a force of nature. His descendants will be the Davidic kings, each one a "Lion of Judah"—an expression that derives from this verse.

Judah is a lion and Benjamin a ravenous wolf. These are poetic descriptions of fierce warrior tribes in the Middle East. This is how one still praises a man in the tribal cultures of this region: he is fierce as a lion or a wolf, and his enemies are defenseless prey—terms of high praise in a culture that values the warrior's art.

This ancient tribal poetry reminds us that Genesis is a book colored by a tribal ethos. The book as a whole is organized as a tribal genealogy that extends from the first ancestors—Adam and Eve—to the eponymous ancestors of the twelve tribes of Israel. The repeating formula "These are the generations of X" is part of the book's connective thread. Again and again the stories focus on threats to the continuity of the tribal family, starting with the threat of death to Adam and Eve in the Garden of Eden, then the murderous relations among their children and descendants (Cain, Lamech, the Flood generation), and most abundantly, the many the threats to the patriarchal families—barrenness and abductions of the matriarchs, deaths or near-deaths of sons, and the final descent of the extended family into Egypt. Genesis focuses on the genealogical tree that culminates in the tribes of Israel, and the trouble that this family faces along the way.

Literary Sources

The major portion of Genesis was written in a dialect that we call classical Biblical Hebrew. From clues of grammar, style, and content, scholars have been able to identify three literary sources for most of Genesis.[2] The three major sources—known as the Yahwist (J), the Elohist (E), and the Priestly source (P)—were carefully combined by one or more editors and later supplemented by some additional material (e.g., the battle with foreign kings in Genesis 14) to yield the final book of Genesis. Each of the major sources is an anthology of traditions featuring the ancestors of the people of Israel, who are bound together by the chain of genealogies. Two of the sources—J and P—begin with the creation of the world, and the other—E—begins with Abraham. Each of these sources continues through the other books of the Pentateuch.

Let us dip into the sources in Genesis to get a sense of their distinctive styles and outlook. Two versions of the Flood—from J and P—have been edited together in Genesis 6–9. Both introductions to the Flood have been preserved intact at the beginning of the story, one version following the other. The two introductions present subtly different perspectives on God's reason for bringing the Flood. (The words in brackets below are harmonizations that were added by the editor who joined the two sources together.)

J

Yahweh saw how great was the evil of man on the earth, for every design of their hearts was only evil all day long. Yahweh regretted that he had made man on the earth, and his heart was pained. Yahweh said, "I shall wipe out man, [whom I created,] from the face of the soil, [from man to land animals to crawling creatures to the birds of heaven,] for I regret that I made them." But Noah found favor in Yahweh's eyes. (Genesis 6:5–8)

P

These are the generations of Noah. Noah was a
man of virtue, blameless in his generation; Noah
walked with God. Noah fathered three sons, Shem,
Ham, and Japheth. Now the earth was ruined
before God, for the earth was filled with violence.
God saw the earth, and behold, it was ruined, for
all flesh had ruined its way on earth. God said to
Noah, "The end of all flesh has come before me, for
the earth is filled with violence because of them.
I shall soon ruin them on the earth." (Genesis
6:9–13)

Notice that the two introductions are independent,
each with its own beginning, and they cover much the
same ground—God's perception that things on earth
have gone wrong, his decision to destroy all life with
the Flood, and the exceptional status of Noah, who
will be spared from destruction. Since the reference to
Noah occurs at the end of the J section and at the beginning of the P section, it was a simple editorial decision to have the J section come first when the two texts
were combined.

Even though these two introductions are equivalent
in content, there are subtle distinctions in the character of God and his motive for sending the Flood. An
initial difference is the name of God—in the J section
he is called by the name Yahweh, while in the P account he is referred to by the generic title, God. This
difference corresponds to the long-term theological

plot in the two sources, for in J the deity is called Yahweh from the beginning of Creation (Genesis 2:4), and humans begin to worship him by that name at the time of Enosh (Genesis 4:26). In P the deity is called God beginning with Creation (Genesis 1:1) until the time of Moses, when God reveals his true name, Yahweh (Exodus 6:2–3).

But the divine names are not the only or most important difference. In J Yahweh is a God who is subject to strong emotions—"Yahweh regretted that he had made man on the earth, and his heart was pained." He is heartbroken that his prize creations—humans—have gone wrong, "for every design of their hearts was only evil all day long." The evil of humans is a terrible blow to Yahweh, and he responds with a forceful decision, "I shall wipe out man . . . from the face of the soil." The words "man" (*'adam*) and "soil" (*'adamah*) are related by a deliberate wordplay, for in the Garden of Eden story *'adam* was made from the *'adamah*, and when he dies he returns to the soil. But now Yahweh decides to end this cycle of life and death with a decisive destruction. And yet immediately after Yahweh announces his pained decision, we are told that this will not be a final end, for "Noah (*noah*) found favor (*hen*) in Yahweh's eyes." Through this wordplay—the consonants of Noah's name (*nh*) are reversed to yield "favor" (*hn*)—we find that Yahweh's initial sight of human evil is now modified by his sight of Noah's goodness. Because of his delight in Noah, humans will be saved from total destruction. Yahweh's agonized response to human evil is balanced by his favor for the one good man. He is moved by regret, wrath, compassion, and delight.

Notice that the concept of humans in J is starkly realistic, harboring no illusions about human perfectibility. Yahweh sees the human heart with all its flaws: "every design of their hearts was only evil all day long." At the end of the J Flood story, Yahweh sees that humans are still and always evil: "the designs of man's heart are evil from their youth" (Genesis 8:21). And yet, in spite of the deep-rooted evil of humans, Yahweh promises, "Never again shall I destroy all life as I have done." Humans are corrupt and flawed creatures, but Yahweh learns to live with them, warts and all. This is a dark view of human nature, which is both disturbing and profound. Even the good man, Noah, is flawed—in the next story he gets drunk and passes out naked (Genesis 9:21).

Are humans really relentlessly evil? Does Yahweh suffer our existence merely because of his compassion, or because he feels responsible for having created us? This is a dark realism—not unlike the later view of Ecclesiastes—a view of reality that is suffused with pain, ambiguity, and complicated morality. The character of Yahweh has depths of which we see only hints, and the reality that he created is ambiguous and often deadly.

In contrast, the P Flood story portrays a God without emotion or regret. He is a transcendent deity who sees the cosmos as a whole and who is not focused on the human heart. This account is less anthropocentric, and its concept of God is less anthropomorphic. When God "sees" the ruined earth, the consequences unfold from this cosmic condition, and not from any emotional response: "God saw the earth, and behold, it was ruined, for all flesh had ruined its way on earth." His perspective takes in "the earth" and "all flesh," not just humans. The text is not clear on how "all flesh had ruined its way," but the earth is now "filled with violence because of them." As a result of this perception of global violence and ruin, God announces the necessary consequence: "The end of all flesh has come before me, for the earth is filled with violence because of them. I shall soon ruin them on the earth." Since all flesh has "ruined its way" and "ruined" the earth, God will redirect this ruin back at all flesh. The wordplay on different forms of the word "ruin" (*šḥt*) connects the problem to its consequence, from ruin to ruin. The "end of all flesh" is not a divine decision or emotional response, but a necessity, a verdict that has "come before me."

This is not a God of regret, wrath, or compassion, but a God who calmly sets out to repair the broken structure of the cosmos. To cleanse the earth of violence and ruin, he returns the physical cosmos to a watery chaos, as it was before Creation. The Flood in P is a reversion to primeval chaos—whereas in J it is a long rainstorm. The waters of the Flood cleanse the earth, washing away its ruin, whereupon God creates the world anew, with Noah as the new Adam. After the Flood God repeats the primeval command to "Be fruitful and multiply and fill the earth" (Genesis 9:1, echoing Genesis 1:28).

Humans are not the center of God's concern in the P account; rather, the harmonious order of the cosmos is his focus. If the earth has to return to watery chaos to cleanse it of violence and ruin, so be it. He will destroy it and start again. But Noah, who is "blameless in his generation," is not ruined, so he does not need to be washed away. God's decision to save Noah is as logical as is his destruction of all the violent creatures on earth. The order of things must be maintained in its goodness and purity, and so the impure, the ruined, and the violent must be destroyed in order that creation may be restored to its pristine order. This is a view of reality as an ordered structure in which all things have their place, and God is the prime mover of the desired state of order. This is a world that P—identifiable as a priest—participates in as a teacher and guardian of God's law on earth. The law serves to maintain the proper order of the cosmos.

The J and P introductions to the Flood illustrate well the style and the cosmological visions of the two sources. P's is a world—and a narrative—of clarity, order, and nested hierarchy. J's is a world of emotions, ambiguity, and ethical complexity. P portrays a transcendental God, a cosmic deity, while J portrays a deity with the human traits of regret, anger, compassion, and delight. These are different conceptions of reality and different conceptions of God and humans. When joined together, the Flood story and Genesis as a whole portray a multifaceted picture of reality, shot through with contradictions and a lingering sense of mystery.

When the editor combined the two accounts, he (not likely a "she" in this patriarchal world) inserted a few P-style words and phrases to the J text. The phrase "whom I created" uses the characteristic term in P for "created" (*br'*), and the list of creatures, "from man to land animals to crawling creatures to the birds of heaven," also draws on P diction. By adding these few words, the editor harmonized the two accounts, expanding J's focus from humans to all creatures and binding it to the P account of Creation. The two stories and sources have become one, and the text of Genesis has become that much more dense, complicated, and enigmatic. The combination of sources, as we will see later, creates a need for interpretation, in order to make sense of these internal contradictions. Genesis is a palimpsest, composed of different sources and texts, from different times and with different philosophies. With effort we can hear the distinctive voices of its constituent texts, and perceive their nuanced—and often differing—perceptions of reality.

Ancient Backgrounds

The sources and their combination are the end of a long process in the genesis of Genesis. Many of the stories in the literary sources have their roots in older oral and written traditions. For instance, the stories of the Flood and Creation have analogues and antecedents in other traditions from Israel and the ancient Near East. The stories of Genesis are part of the larger matrix of ancient Near Eastern myth and epic. Many of these old traditions have been rediscovered during the last two centuries of archaeological excavations. We now have thousands of texts from Mesopotamia, Canaan, Egypt, and other neighboring lands, and many shed light on the backgrounds of the Genesis narratives.

These ancient traditions were transmitted across cultures and languages by journeying traders, scribes, seers, and storytellers, and eventually became native to Israelite culture and religion. A couple of glimpses of the Israelite transmission of these oral traditions are given in the old poems "The Song of Moses" and "The Song of Deborah":

> Remember the days of old,
>> Consider the years of ancient generations.
> Ask your father, and he will tell you,
>> Your elders, and they will inform you.
>>>> (Deuteronomy 32:8)

> To the sound of (?),[3] by the watering holes,
>> There they recite the righteous deeds of Yahweh
>> The righteous deeds of his villagers in Israel.
>>>> (Judges 5:11)

These poems evoke the family, tribal, and village settings of oral traditions of the ancient past. The stories of Genesis are derived from these ancient traditions, transmitted through generations, recounted by fathers, elders, travelers, and bards who were the authoritative voices of tradition.

Let us turn to the Flood story on another level, now with an eye to its ancient background in oral and written traditions. There are several versions of the Babylonian Flood story, all of which are older than Genesis—the oldest Babylonian version is from around 1800 BCE, roughly a thousand years earlier than the J source. Most scholars agree that the biblical versions are descended from the Babylonian versions, presumably mediated by oral traditions. Once it was transmitted on Israelite soil—by fathers, elders, travelers, bards, and scribes—it became adapted to Israelite tradition.

The version of the Flood in tablet XI of the Standard Babylonian epic of *Gilgamesh* (ca. 1100 BCE) has many similarities to the J Flood story. When the Flood ceases, the Babylonian Flood hero (named Utnapishtim) is in his ark, which rests atop Mount Nimush in northern Mesopotamia:

> When the seventh day arrived—
> I brought out a dove, setting it free:
>> off went the dove.
>> No perch was available for it and it came back
>> to [me.]
> I brought out a swallow, setting it free:
>> off went the swallow.
>> No perch was available for it and it came back
>> to me.

I brought out a raven, setting it free:
>   off went the raven and it saw the waters
>   receding.
>   It was eating, bobbing up and down, it did not
>   come back to me.
> I brought out an offering and sacrificed to the four
>   winds of the earth,
>   I strewed incense on the peak of the mountain.
>   (*Gilgamesh* XI.148–58)[4]

In this scene, the Flood hero sends out three birds to see if the waters have abated and then offers a sacrifice in thanks to the gods. Noah does much the same thing from his ark on top of the mountains of Ararat, some distance north of Mount Nimush:

> At the end of forty days, Noah opened the window of the ark that he had made. He sent out a raven, and it went back and forth until the water had dried on the earth. He sent out a dove that was with him to see if the water had subsided on the face of the soil. But the dove did not find a place to rest its feet, so it returned to him on the ark, for the water still covered the whole face of the earth. He reached out his hand and caught it and brought it back into the ark. He waited another seven days and again sent the dove from the ark. The dove returned to him toward evening, and there in its beak was a plucked olive leaf, and Noah knew that the water had subsided on the face of the earth. He waited another seven days and sent

out the dove, but it did not return to him again. . . .
He took one of every clean animal and every clean
bird and offered burnt offerings on the altar. (Genesis 8:6–12, 20)

Noah sends a single raven and then a dove three
times—which differs from Utnapishtim's sequence of
dove, swallow, and raven—but the motif of sending
birds to see if the waters have abated is the same. It
derives from a trick of ancient mariners to see if a ship
is close to land. But in this case, from the top of a
mountain, Utnapishtim and Noah could have simply
looked out the window: the birds are not strictly necessary. The sending of the birds is a colorful motif
that slows down the action—thereby creating suspense—and vividly depicts the passage of time. The
returning dove in Genesis, a "plucked olive leaf" in its
beak, offers a miniature vision of life reborn, just as
Utnapishtim's raven, who "saw the waters receding . . .
eating, bobbing up and down," shows that life will
go on.

There are also other differences between the two
stories—one is poetry, the other prose; in one the
Flood lasts seven days, and in the other forty days.
More importantly, the cause of the Flood is different.
In the Babylonian story the god Enlil sends the Flood
to destroy humans because they are too numerous and
noisy, whereas in the J story Yahweh sends the Flood to
destroy humans because they are evil. There are many
gods involved in the Babylonian Flood versus one God

in the biblical story. Yet in spite of these differences, many of the details of plot, character, conflict, and setting are strikingly similar. The similarities—in conjunction with the closeness of the two cultures—indicate that the Flood story in Genesis descends from an older family of stories.

Other stories and motifs—including the Garden of Eden story—also have old roots in Israelite and ancient Near Eastern traditions. The book of Ezekiel has a story of sin and punishment in the Garden of Eden that significantly differs from the story in Genesis, indicating that the story existed in multiple oral versions. Ezekiel recites a dirge over the king of Tyre, addressing him as if he were the original cherub (a sphinx-like creature) in the Garden of Eden:

> [You were] full of wisdom and perfect in beauty;
> You were in Eden, the garden of God.
> Every precious stone was your hedge:
> Carnelian, chrysolite, and diamond,
> Beryl, onyx, and jasper,
> Sapphire, turquoise, and emerald ...
> I placed you on the holy mountain of God ...
> You walked among the stones of fire.
> You were righteous in your ways
> From the day you were created,
> Until evil was found in you ...
> So I cast you out from the mountain of God,
> And I destroyed you, O shielding cherub.
>   (Ezekiel 28:12–16)

According to this story, God cast down the proud cherub from the Garden of Eden, which is on the mountain of God, and destroyed him. Ezekiel uses this story to illustrate the fate of the recently deceased king of Tyre. This is a different Garden of Eden story than in Genesis, but it shares many of the same motifs and themes—cherubs, wisdom, transgression, and exile from the Garden of Eden. In Genesis, God assigns cherubs to guard the way to the Garden of Eden so that humans cannot return (Genesis 3:24), but here the cherub is the main character in the Garden, and he is cast out and destroyed. Notice also that in Genesis there are precious stones outside of Eden (in the land of Havilah, Genesis 2:11–12), but in Ezekiel the precious stones are in Eden. There are also other variations of this motif—there are precious stones at God's abode at the top of Mount Sinai (Exodus 24:10), and there are trees made of precious stones in a divine garden in *Gilgamesh* IX.172–94. The circulation of stories about the Garden of Eden seems to have included a wider diversity than Genesis allows us to see. In other words, the story of primal transgression in the Garden of Eden belongs to a wider family of stories in Israel and its environs.[5]

There are also many stories of Creation—both within and without the Bible—that show that the Creation accounts in Genesis belong to a wider family of stories. To choose one example from many, consider this excerpt from a Babylonian story of Creation, featuring the creator-god Marduk:

All the world was sea, the spring in the midst of the
    sea was only a channel. . . .
Marduk tied together a raft on the face of the
    waters,
He created dirt and heaped it on the raft.
In order to settle the gods in a comfortable
    dwelling,
He created humankind,
(The goddess) Aruru created the seed of
    humankind with him.
He created the wild animals, the living creatures of
    the open country.
He created and put in place the Tigris and
    Euphrates rivers,
He pronounced their names with favor.
He created the dry rush, the pulpy reed, the marsh,
    the reed thicket, the stand of reeds,
    the vegetation of the open country. . . .
[He laid bricks], he created the brick mold.
[He built cities], he founded settlements.
    ("Marduk, Creator of the World," lines 10–38)[6]

In this story the primeval scene is water ("All the world
was sea"), as in Genesis 1 ("darkness covered the face of
the ocean"). Marduk creates dirt and makes dry land
on the waters, comparable to God's work of creation
on the third day ("Let the water below heaven gather
together into one pool, so that dry land may appear").
Of course, piling dirt on a raft is less elegant than the
creation by word in Genesis 1, but the result is simi-

lar—dry land above the primeval water. Marduk creates humans next, "in order to settle the gods in a comfortable dwelling." This is similar to the role of Adam in Eden, whose task is to tend the divine garden ("He placed him in the Garden of Eden to work it and to guard it"). In the Babylonian myth, humans are the first creatures created, followed by all the animals, as in the Garden of Eden creation story (but unlike Genesis 1). Marduk ends by building cities, which in the biblical accounts are built by people, not by God. But the systematic divine creation of an orderly world is a common pattern, with all things in their place.

As this Babylonian myth indicates, the stories of Creation in Genesis belong to a wider family of creation traditions.[7] But the stories in Genesis are not mere repetitions of the older traditions; they take the old motifs and stories and reorient them to create distinctive ways of understanding and representing reality. Let us look more closely at these new beginnings.

In the Beginning

In the English of the King James Version, Genesis begins with the sonorous words "In the beginning." Notice that the syllable "in" occurs three times. In Hebrew, too, the beginning uses the effect of the repetition of sound: *bereshit bara*, where *bere* and *bara* echo each other. The whole account in Hebrew is filled with echoing repetitions, including whole phrases—"and it was so," "evening and morning," "and it was good"—which lends a sense of structure and harmony to the whole.

The Creation account in Genesis 1:1–2:3 was written by P, an Israelite priest, around the sixth century BCE.[8] It was prefixed to the whole book by an editor who combined the P source with the earlier sources. It is the prerogative of the editor to organize the whole, to put his mark on the final scroll. Genesis begins with a text that is leagues away conceptually from the old tribal poem of Genesis 49. Creation in Genesis 1 is a magnificent cosmological system, with inner symmetries and repetitions that create order in the text and in the cosmos. In the schema below, notice both the sequential (vertical) and thematic (horizontal) design in the creation of the universe:

Initial chaos: Water, darkness,
submerged earth, God's wind

Day 1: Creation of light	Day 4: Creation of sun, moon, and stars
Day 2: Creation of heaven, separation of waters	Day 5: Creation of water and sky creatures
Day 3: Creation of dry land and vegetation	Day 6: Creation of land creatures and humans

Day 7: Completed cosmos: God rests

Let us unpack this literary-cosmological design. First, there is a stylistic, temporal, and conceptual framing by the initial chaos and the completed cosmos.

The initial chaos consists of four primeval elements: water, darkness, submerged earth, and God's wind:

> In the beginning, when God created heaven and earth—the earth was a formless chaos, darkness covered the face of the ocean, and a wind from God was soaring over the face of the water. (Genesis 1:1–2)

By the seventh day there are myriad created things in heaven and earth:

> Now heaven and earth and all their array were complete. . . . God blessed the seventh day and made it holy, for on it he rested from all his work that God created. (Genesis 2:1–3)

The repetitions of "heaven and earth" and "God created" at the beginning and end bracket the creation account. Conceptually, the picture of "heaven and earth" has changed utterly—at the beginning it is chaotic, and at the end it is complete. God's rest and his blessing of the seventh day contrast with the timeless chaos of the primeval state. Now there is a proper order of time and space, and there is a structured universe that God affirms as "very good." The progression from chaos to a divinely ordered cosmos is finished.

In the six days between the primeval chaos and the completed cosmos, there are two thematically aligned series of three days. During the first three days God separates and supplements the primeval elements to make parts of the created cosmos. During the second series of three days, God fills these newly created cosmic domains with their appropriate inhabitants. Let us look at the creative works of these two series of days.

On the first day God creates light. The creation of light and the separation of light from darkness yield the orderly progression of day and night—this is the creation of time. The temporal order of the cosmos begins by alternating primeval darkness with the beneficent light ("it was good"). Before this there was no time, no change, only the formless flux of chaos.

The creation of light and the new order of time is supplemented and completed on the fourth day, when God creates the heavenly bodies—the sun, moon, and stars:

> God set them in the vault of heaven to light up the earth, to rule the day and the night, and to separate the light from the darkness. (Genesis 1:17–18)

These heavenly bodies are created as instruments of light and time, "to rule" the progression of day and night. They also serve as "signs for the festivals, the days, and the years" (1:14), which is another part of their function as instruments of time. With the creation of the heavenly bodies, the temporal order of the cosmos is set. God's creations on the fourth day complete his creative work on the first day.

On the second day God creates the vault of heaven and separates "the water below the vault from the water above the vault" (1:7). By creating the vault of heaven to divide the primeval waters, God creates difference between above and below—this is the creation of space. Now there are different spatial domains—the celestial waters above the vault, the vault of heaven, the air beneath the vault, and the terrestrial waters. Just as the primeval darkness was separated and integrated into the order of time, so now the primeval waters are separated and integrated into the newly created order of space. The chaotic waters, like the primeval darkness, are "domesticated" into useful features of the ordered universe.

The new domains of space are complemented and completed on the fifth day, when God populates the terrestrial water and the air with living creatures: "Let the waters teem with teeming life, and let birds fly over the earth beneath the vault of heaven" (1:20). The creatures made on the fifth day inhabit the cosmic spaces created on the second day.

On the third day—the end of the first series of days—there are two separate acts of creation, as there are on the corresponding sixth day. God separates and gathers the terrestrial waters to create dry land, and he commands the earth to bear vegetation. Now the fruitful earth is ready to nourish living creatures, which accordingly God creates on the sixth day. First he creates land animals, and then he creates humans:

God said, "Let the earth yield every kind of living creature—domestic animals, crawling creatures, and wild animals of every kind." And it was so. . . .

God said, "Let us make humans in our image, according to our likeness, so that they may rule the fish of the sea, the birds of heaven, and the animals, and every crawling creature on earth." (Genesis 1:24, 26)

The spatial domain of the dry land is now inhabited by land animals of every kind and by humans. The humans—male and female—are created in the image of God. As God's images and representatives on earth, the humans are charged to rule the other animals of land, sea, and sky. Just as the heavenly bodies are created to rule time, so humans are created to rule the earth and all living creatures. The creatures made on the sixth day inhabit the dry land and eat the vegetation created on the third day. The final creation, humans, completes the hierarchical structure of the ordered cosmos.

This account of Creation is a coherent cosmological system, which derives the universe from a few basic elements. It shows how God created the cosmos as a majestic, rationally ordered, and morally good universe. God's creation of humans to rule as his earthly "image" is a capstone to the wholeness and goodness of the created order. The cosmos is complete, the Sabbath is its holy sign, and God is content with the world. He sees that everything in it is "very good" (1:31).

In its elaborate symmetries, coherent structure, and majestic style, this Creation account is unique in the ancient world. It expresses a view of reality that has a transcendent axis—since God transcends the natural world—and that emphasizes the goodness of the world. Nothing in the cosmos is random or incomplete—God has seen to the harmonious order of all space and time. The potential harm of primeval chaos has been neutralized within the positive structures of reality. Even gender relationships are balanced and harmonious, since both "male and female" are created "in the image of God," and are equally vested with blessings and responsibilities. It is a good world, created by a beneficent and omnipotent God. The cosmos is both rational and moral, and in it humans have a noble place.

The Creation account itself is a powerful blend of natural science and theology, which transforms the older mythic motifs of creation into a new vehicle of thought. The four primeval elements—darkness, water, earth, wind—are reminiscent of older Egyptian and Babylonian myth. The orderly structure of Creation is also reminiscent of early Greek philosophical speculation about the universe. The account is a narrative, telling the story of Creation in seven days, but there is no dramatic tension, character development, or conflict. There is a deliberate mention of the "great dragons" of the sea (Genesis 1:21), but they are not adversaries—as they are in earlier myths—only a species of sea creature that God creates. In this implicit "taming" of the dragons, we see another transformation of potential chaos into the natural order of the cosmos. Reality has a structure that is orderly and philosophical, at once majestic and reasoned. It is a unique view of reality as an intricate divine order, and it has shaped our sensibility of the universe ever since.

Adam and Eve

One of the complications of Genesis is that is has two versions of Creation. As soon as the first account ends, a second account begins, with a different sequence of creation: first man, then the Garden of Eden, then animals, and finally woman. This is the J story of human origins and transgression in the Garden of Eden. The editor who combined the two accounts added a harmonizing transition by combining the divine names of the P and J sources into a double name, God Yahweh:

> On the day God Yahweh made earth and heaven—
> when wild plants of the field were not on the earth,
> when grasses of the field had not yet grown, for
> God Yahweh had not sent rain on the earth, and
> there was no man to work the soil, though a flood
> used to rise from the earth and water the whole
> surface of the soil—God Yahweh formed a man
> from the dust of the soil. (Genesis 2:4–7)

The J source is earlier than the P source,[9] and gives an independent story. Notice that it has its own beginning and its own description of the initial chaos— an agricultural chaos that lacks plants, rain, or humans—before God Yahweh creates the present world order. He first creates man, in contrast to Genesis 1, where light was created first and humans were created last. For early interpreters, the odd repetition of God's creative works in the two sections—in a different order and with different nuances and consequences—is a troublesome feature that calls for subtle interpretation. Usually the second Creation account is read as a flashback or elaboration of the sixth day of Creation, when animals and humans were created. But the different order and different motivations are a lingering problem.

In the Garden of Eden story, the first man is created to work the soil, which resolves one of the primeval absences: "there was no man to work the soil" (2:5). Then God Yahweh plants the Garden of Eden and "placed him in the Garden of Eden to work it and to guard it" (2:15). This is man's initial destiny. Later, after he disobeys God Yahweh's command and eats the fruit of the Tree of the Knowledge of Good and Evil, the man will have to work the soil outside of the Garden, and the earth will henceforth withhold its fruit. Adam's toil will be harsh and painful, until he returns to the soil—here is the end of the wordplay between "man" (*'adam*) and "soil" (*'adamah*). In contrast to the divine blessings of Genesis 1, Adam is now subject to a powerful curse. God says:

> Cursed be the soil because of you. In painful labor you shall eat from it all the days of your life. Thorns

and thistles it shall sprout for you, and you shall eat the grasses of the field. By the sweat of your brow you shall eat bread, until you return to the soil, for from it you were taken. For you are dust, and to dust you shall return. (Genesis 3:17–19)

This picture of man's existence—colored by the cursed soil, painful labor, and death—corresponds to the stark realism of J's Flood story (see above). Reality is harsh and unforgiving, a life of subsistence agriculture and the looming consciousness of death. The ease and innocence of life in paradise is no more—henceforth life is, in Thomas Hobbes's famous phrase, nasty, brutish, and short.

And yet, man—in the broad sense of "human," since at this point there is male and female—now possesses "the knowledge of good and evil," which makes humans "like gods." This newly attained knowledge seems to consist of varying degrees of moral knowledge, sexual awareness, and individual self-consciousness. It permanently elevates the status of humans, even as it results in exile from paradise. The resulting picture of reality is therefore complicated—humans gain a measure of wisdom, but lose paradise. Knowledge and self-consciousness are a counterbalance to the harsh life outside of Eden, and to some extent redeem the loss. The result is an ambiguous picture of reality, shot through with knowledge, mortality, joy, and suffering.

Overlaid on this complex view of life, there is a distinctive view of gender in the J story. Because Eve listened to the snake and chose to disobey the divine command and brought her husband into disobedience too, God curses her:

> I will greatly multiply your pain from pregnancy—
> in pain you shall bear children. You shall desire
> your husband, and he shall rule over you. (Genesis
> 3:16)

Women are now cursed with painful labor, but in childbirth rather than agriculture. Gender roles are differentiated here, but both have their burdens. As a punishment and reversal of Eve's desire for the forbidden fruit, which she gave to her husband to eat, henceforth wives shall desire their husbands, and the husband shall rule. Eve's punishments are attuned to her culpable acts in the Garden. Her desire for the forbidden fruit—which seems to imply both sexual and divine knowledge—is turned into desire for her husband in a patriarchal hierarchy. The origin of different gender roles, which reverse the original harmony of Adam and Eve in the Garden, are consequences of Eve's intelligent disobedience.

The Garden of Eden story is a tale of how the world and humans came into their present form.[10] It bears a different emotional and conceptual load than the account of origins in Genesis 1. This is one of the accidental virtues of the combination of the P and J sources in

Genesis—the world is both "very good" and very pain-ful, and humans are both the pinnacle of creation and creatures that bear great suffering. There is a harsh real-ism in the Garden of Eden story that balances the cos-mic harmony of the P Creation account. In the combi-nation of accounts, humans are both masters and laborers, and God is the giver of blessings and curses.

The Garden of Eden story depicts a reality that is very earthly and—from the human point of view—very imperfect. Humans become "like gods" by gaining the knowledge of good and evil, but the contents of this knowledge are ambiguous and double-edged. Hu-mans now are more than they were before, but their increased knowledge entails a loss of innocence and an exile from paradise. In one sense it is a story of growing up—from a state of childhood innocence and depen-dence to the sorrows and independence of adulthood. In this view of reality, humans are condemned to be free—but are subject to strict limits. We take pride in our God-like knowledge, and even in our capacity to disobey God's command, but it is a harsh world that we inhabit and bequeath to our children.

God is both gracious and punishing—he creates, feels compassion ("It is not good for the man to be alone"), makes clothes, and finally expels humans. We must fear and respect him. Yet he is not the transcen-dent and cosmic God of Genesis 1. He walks and talks in the Garden, and he even makes mistakes (remember that the animals are not the solution to Adam's loneliness, so God created Eve). The descendants of Adam and Eve must make their way together in a difficult world, guided by a spark of divine knowledge.

Genesis was born from a combination of stories and sources that derived from the traditions of ancient lore. It is a plural and complex book, which corresponds to a multifarious world. Once Genesis was born, its powerful meanings coalesced in different ways according to new backgrounds and perspectives. Within a few generations, the carefully composed senses of the text yielded to a view of Genesis as a perfect book—a Holy Scripture—that both reveals and conceals divine secrets.

The Rise of the Figural Sense

CHAPTER 2

"He read it aloud in the public square before the
Water Gate from dawn to midday, to the men,
women, and those who could understand."

Giving the Meaning

Ever since its birth, the book of Genesis has attracted interpreters of every stripe. For various reasons—including its laconic style, its complex compositional history, and its religious content—it requires interpretation. From our first glimpse of Genesis as a book in the public domain, it is an interpreted text. This event is presented in the book of Nehemiah, from the fifth century BCE:

> Ezra the priest brought the Torah to the congregation—the men, women, and all who could understand—on the first day of the seventh month. He read it aloud in the public square before the Water Gate from dawn to midday, to the men, women, and those who could understand. The ears of all the people were attentive. . . . The Levites explained the Torah to the people while the people stood. They read aloud precisely from the Book of the Torah of God, and they gave the meaning, so that they would understand the reading. (Nehemiah 8:2–8)

That the Torah (literally, "teaching" or "law") includes Genesis is clear from the next chapter, where the Levites summarize and interpret Genesis, beginning with "You created the heavens" (Nehemiah 9:6–8). In the scene of Ezra reading the Torah, notice the emphasis on the importance of explaining and understanding the Torah. The word "understand, explain" (*yabin*) occurs four times (in different forms) in this passage. The phrases "all who could understand," "those who could understand," and "so that they would understand" echo in this scene. Reading and interpreting the Torah are interrelated tasks—it requires people "who could understand" and interpreters who can "explain ... read precisely ... [and] give the meaning." Reading the biblical text is not enough; it takes an interpreter and a willing audience to make understanding happen.

Why is interpretation so necessary? There are a number of reasons, rooted in the antiquity, authority, and complexity of the text.[1] The scene of the first public reading of the Torah portrays an event on New Year's Day (Rosh Hashanah) in the middle of the fifth century BCE. This is a good day for a new beginning, a new revelation of God's Torah. The event—whether it really happened this way is not particularly important, and it is probably embellished anyway—is hundreds of years after the composition of the earlier sources of Genesis. By then many Hebrew words, expressions, and grammatical constructions had already become obscure and half-forgotten. So the language of the book often requires interpretation.

As we have seen, the additive nature of each source and the combination of the sources created many inconsistencies and puzzles in the text that also beg for interpretation. Some of these notorious puzzles, faced alike by early and modern interpreters, include the following: Why are humans and animals created twice?

Who are the other people that Cain is afraid will kill him? (Surely not Adam and Eve, his father and mother.) Who was Cain's wife? (Was she his sister?) How many animals came to Noah in the ark—two of each animal or seven pair of the clean animals and one pair of the unclean animals? Did Methuselah drown in the Flood? Why was Hagar expelled twice? Why was Beersheba founded twice? Why did Jacob name Bethel twice? These and many other puzzles—which originate in the complicated compositional history of Genesis—require interpretation.

Another weighty motive for interpretation is the drive to make the text relevant for the present. If Genesis is part of "the Torah of God" (Nehemiah 8:8), its subject matter should never be trivial. But what, then, is one to make of the many lists and genealogies? They seem to be antiquarian details. Perhaps most difficult is the problem of Jacob's trickery—how can deceiving one's old blind father be an edifying example for the present? Not to mention the strange story of the Sons of God having sex with human women. How and why should we understand the relevance of these stories? If these texts are worthy of being part of God's Torah, then surely they must be important and meaningful somehow. It takes an interpreter who wields authority and respect to explain how and why these texts are relevant for the present.

These reasons all circle around a more general motive for interpretation, which was strongly felt by early interpreters. If Genesis is part of "the Torah of God," this seems to imply that God has authorized—perhaps even authored—this book. When Moses received the law from God at Mount Sinai, we are told that God spoke to him directly. Over and over the text says, "Yahweh said to Moses," or "God spoke all these words." If God directly instructed Moses in the law (= Torah), then we might expect the other parts of the Torah to be divinely revealed or sanctioned as well. In other words, Genesis, as part of "the Torah of God," came to be treated as a divine revelation, just like the commandments and laws. As such, there can be no trivial or meaningless features in Genesis. This motive for interpretation is fundamental—everything in Genesis derives from God, and everything must therefore be significant.

Four Assumptions

Let us dwell for a moment on these interrelated motives for interpretation. In his marvelous book *The Bible As It Was*, James Kugel distills these motives into four assumptions that became widespread in the generations and centuries after the Torah was "published" (that is, made public) by the Water Gate in Jerusalem.[2] These four assumptions undergird all the different forms of early biblical interpretation and also undergird the views of reality that came to prevail in this era. The four assumptions are that the Bible is cryptic, relevant, perfect, and divine.

1. Cryptic

It doesn't take much effort to find a cryptic passage in Genesis. But the idea that Genesis is cryptic *by design* is a more far-reaching assumption. A cryptic text has coded or hidden meanings, which it is the task of the interpreter to uncover. For many interpreters, from antiquity to the present, the interpretation of Genesis is a hunt for hidden meanings, which are flagged by obscurities in the text.

Consider, for example, the brief account of the life of Enoch in the genealogy from Adam to Noah.

> Enoch lived 65 years and fathered Methuselah. After he fathered Methuselah, Enoch walked with God for 300 years. He fathered sons and daughters. All the days of Enoch were 365 years. And Enoch walked with God and then was no more, for God took him. (Genesis 5:21–24)

What does it mean to say that "Enoch walked with God and then was no more, for God took him"? This is a genuinely cryptic passage, and it is unclear what Genesis means. It seems that Enoch was a righteous man—this is what "walking with God" means elsewhere (e.g., Noah in Genesis 6:9, Abraham in Genesis 17:1)—whom God may have taken up to heaven (compare Elijah's ascent to heaven in 2 Kings 2:11). But the text doesn't say this explicitly—it doesn't tell us the whole story. The job of the biblical interpreter, like that of a detective, is to ferret out the whole story from hints in the text.

In the third century BCE someone wrote a book purportedly by Enoch, in which Enoch tells his whole story. In his memoir we learn that he was a righteous man who ascended to heaven and walked with angels. Enoch is part prophet and part visionary seer, who warns the people in the generations before the Flood to be righteous or face divine punishment. He is granted visions of heaven, and he sees the places of reward and punishment after death. He says to his son, Methuselah:

> The vision of heaven was shown to me,
> and from the words of the watchers and holy ones
>   I have learned everything,
> and in the heavenly tablets I read everything and I
>   understood.
>
> (1 Enoch 93:2)[3]

Enoch is not only a righteous man who has traveled with angels (these are "the watchers and holy ones"), but he also knows how to read and understand the heavenly tablets. His explanation of his own cryptic story in Genesis is reliable, since he was there. And he himself is a wise and divinely authorized interpreter of divine texts.

Another example of a cryptic passage in Genesis shows how early interpreters not only filled in gaps and obscurities in the text, but also generated new religious ideas. The following passage is from "The Blessing of Jacob," where Jacob blesses his son Judah with a prophecy of a glorious future:

The scepter shall not depart from Judah
Nor the staff from between his feet,
So that tribute may come to him,
And the obedience of nations shall be his.

(Genesis 49:10)

This passage is cryptic for two reasons. First, some of the language is obscure or archaic. The clause "So that tribute may come to him" has an unusual preposition (*'ad ki* usually means "until," and rarely means "so that"). The sequence "tribute ... to him" (*šay lo*) is squeezed together into one word in the traditional Hebrew text, yielding *šilo*, as if it were a name, "Shiloh" (as in the city, Shiloh). It looks like this line reads, "Until Shiloh comes to him," which doesn't make sense. These are linguistic obscurities, which occur because "The Blessing of Jacob" is an old poetic text. To the interpreter, these obscurities were hints of deeper meanings.

The second reason that this passage is cryptic has to do with history. For the people of Israel at the time of Ezra and for centuries after, there was no king from the tribe of Judah on the throne. The people were ruled by foreign empires and kings. (The only exception was during the native Hasmonean dynasty in the second and first centuries BCE.) So the scepter *did* depart from Judah! But a prominent prophecy in the Torah of God must be true somehow. Perhaps the clues in the cryptic words can yield the passage's deeper meaning, so that it is not contradicted by historical realities. It is the task of the interpreter to find this deeper cryptic meaning.

According to many interpreters over the years, the hidden meaning of this verse is the promise of a future king from the tribe of Judah, an "anointed one" or *messiah* (the Hebrew word *mašiaḥ*, "anointed one," comes into Greek as "messiah"). The promise of an eternal dynasty is only temporarily interrupted, until the coming of a once-and-future king, whose code name is Shiloh. So a passage from the Dead Sea Scrolls interprets this passage:

> The scepter shall [n]ot depart from the tribe of Judah. . . . Until the messiah of righteousness comes, the branch of David. For the covenant of his people's kingship has been given to him and his descendants for everlasting generations. (*Commentary on Genesis* A [4Q252])[4]

The words "until the messiah of righteousness comes" is an interpretation of the cryptic line of Genesis that seems to say "until Shiloh comes to him." The obscure word Shiloh is read as a secret name of "the messiah of righteousness," who is "the branch of David." This is the Davidic messiah, who will fulfill the prophecy in this verse and return to rule as king and savior. According to this interpretation, the promise of the messiah is an everlasting promise, which cannot fail to happen.

By these interpretive means, the prophecy of the royal Davidic dynasty from the tribe of Judah is transformed into the expectation of the future messiah.

This is a new idea that emerged from the interpretation of this verse, in conjunction with other verses about the eternal covenant with David (e.g., 2 Samuel 7:8–16). This idea became widespread during the postexilic period. The cryptic language and the apparent contradiction with historical reality yielded a new secret—Jacob's blessing to Judah contains the promise of the messianic future. In other words, this cryptic verse gave birth to the concept of the messiah.

2. Relevant

The previous example shows that current relevance was a natural expectation for any Genesis verse. But what about texts that aren't obscure and seem to be antique details, such as lists of people and places? How can such dry facts possibly be relevant to the present? The geographical and genealogical texts posed a challenge to early interpreters, who had to meet the expectation that all biblical texts were, as Paul says, "written down for our instruction" (1 Corinthians 10:11).

Consider the following geographical description of the four rivers that flow from the Garden of Eden:

> The name of the first is Pishon. It circles the whole land of Havilah, where there is gold. The gold of that land is excellent, and bdellium and carnelian are there. The name of the second river is Gihon. It circles the whole land of Cush. The name of the third river is Tigris. It flows east of Assyria. The fourth river is the Euphrates. (Genesis 2:11–14)

This passage gives the Garden of Eden a realistic setting, since the places of Havilah and Cush are well known, as are the rivers Tigris and Euphrates. At the same time the realistic setting is confusing, since these places are nowhere near each other—Havilah is in South Arabia, Cush is in northern Africa, and the Tigris and Euphrates rivers are in Mesopotamia. The passage has a layered effect, suggesting realism while at the same time obscuring it. In this geographical description, Eden seems to have a real location, but it cannot be found on any map. Its geography is a paradox.

This interpretation—the location of Eden as a deliberate paradox—was not available to the early interpreters. For them, the description was self-evidently true. But it was not particularly edifying—since the Garden of Eden is not accessible to humans anyway, its entrance being guarded by fierce sphinx-like creatures (Genesis 3:24). This descriptive list, and others like it, challenge the assumption that everything in Genesis is relevant for the present.

The Hellenistic Jewish interpreter Philo of Alexandria (who we will consider more thoroughly later) took up this challenge and read the passage as a symbolic description not of four rivers, but of the four virtues. The number "four" was the relevant clue. Philo writes:

By these rivers he [Moses] wishes to indicate the particular virtues. These are four in number: wisdom, self-control, courage, justice. The largest river, of which the four are effluences, is generic virtue. . . . [T]he four specific virtues derive from the generic virtue, which like a river irrigates the right conduct of each of them with the abundant flow of noble actions. (*Allegorical Interpretation*, 1.63–64)[5]

Philo here assumes that the geographical description is actually a cryptic text or code that yields a symbolic interpretation as the four cardinal virtues. With this interpretation, the text is shown to be relevant and edifying—it is now an ethical treatise for the improvement of the soul. Every detail of Genesis is written for our instruction, even if it takes profound wisdom to discern its deeper, hidden, edifying meanings.

3. Perfect

It follows from the divine attribution of "the Torah of God" that Genesis must be perfect. This means that it has no internal contradictions and does not conflict with the world outside the text. It must be intelligible, relevant, edifying, and unified in all its parts. Its seeming imperfections are a sign of its cryptic nature, which call out for more intensive interpretation. Its imperfections are only apparent—they are really flags that indicate hidden meanings within, where the wise and authoritative interpreter will find its more perfect sense.

The perfection of Scripture is a reflection of God's perfection, since it is after all his teaching. Inevitably, this assumption of perfection came to include every detail, even the untranslatable features of the text, such as spelling, word order, and grammar. If the Torah is seen as God's own speech, every feature of the book must be significant, perhaps even infinitely significant.

Consider, for instance, the conclusion of the first account of Creation:

> These are the generations of heaven and earth,
> when they were created. (Genesis 2:4)

The formula "These are the generations of . . ." occurs roughly ten times in Genesis, creating an internal structure within the book. The last clause, "when they were created," coming after "heaven and earth," echoes the initial sequence, "God created heaven and earth," in Genesis 1:1, thus framing the whole Creation account.

But a perfect text does not have repetitions that are merely literary or stylistic. To the early interpreters, each word has its own special significance. God does not repeat himself or use rhetorical flourishes; his words must always reveal new meanings. So the Hebrew word *behibbar'am*, "when they were created," was turned around and examined for deeper meanings. The Hebrew of Genesis was originally written without vowel marks (and Torah scrolls are still written without vowels), and so interpreters could, if they wished, focus only on the consonants. According to *Genesis Rabbah*, a compilation of early rabbinic interpretation, one rabbi found the hidden meaning of this word as follows:

Rabbi Joshua Ben-Qorhah said, "*behibbar'am—be'abraham*. It was on account of the merit of Abraham." (*Genesis Rabbah* 12.9)[6]

According to this (rather cryptic) interpretation, the letters of the word *behibbar'am* can be reordered, as one does in a game of Scrabble, to spell *be'abraham*, "for Abraham." In the consonants-only script, *bhbr'm* is reordered as *b'brhm*. The apparently insignificant word yields a deeper meaning—heaven and earth were created for the sake of the righteousness of Abraham. God's creation of the universe was motivated by his knowledge that Abraham, the exemplary man who would be chosen for God's covenant, would live in it someday. The account of Creation now has its perfect meaning revealed. Creation, according to the omnisignificant words of Genesis, anticipates the coming of Abraham. Even repetitions and stylistic flourishes have perfect meanings.

4. Divine

Connected to all of these assumptions is the global assumption that Genesis is, in some sense, divine speech—either authorized or authored by God. This assumption, as we have seen, arises at least in part from the name of the book, the "Torah of God," and the analogy with God's revelation of his laws to Moses. These clues eventually gave rise to the idea that God dictated the entire Torah to Moses on Mount Sinai.

This assumption is made explicit for the first time in the book of Jubilees (written in the second century BCE), which retells and interprets Genesis and Exodus. Jubilees opens with Moses at Mount Sinai, awaiting God's revelation. God commands Moses:

> "Now you write all the words which I will tell you on this mountain: what is first and what is last and what is to come. . . ." Then he said to an angel of the presence, "Dictate to Moses from the beginning of creation." (*Jubilees* 1:26–27)[7]

The angel of the presence takes up this task:

> On the Lord's orders the angel of the presence said to Moses: "Write all the words about the creation—how in six days the Lord God completed all his works, everything that he had created, and kept Sabbath on the seventh day." (Jubilees 2:1)[8]

The angel continues to dictate Genesis, chapter by chapter, but elaborates, embellishes, and abridges the biblical text as he goes. Jubilees depicts the origins of the book of Genesis *and* its interpretation, both of which are revealed to Moses by God through the dictation of the angel of the presence. (The angel later says in Jubilees 6:22, "I have written [this] in the book of the first law," referring back to the biblical text.) The book of Jubilees recounts the book of Genesis, but refashions it in a way that incorporates the interpretations of the Jubilees writer. Genesis and its interpretation are both revealed to Moses at Mount Sinai.

The interpretation of Genesis in Jubilees makes explicit the divine origins of both books in the scene of revelation and writing at Sinai. As a book of divine dictation, Genesis is complete and perfect in itself, but at the same time its perfection and relevance—its true and deeper meanings—must be revealed by an interpreter (in this case an angelic interpreter). According to Jubilees, God revealed the Torah and its interpretation simultaneously at Sinai. (This view later reappears in the rabbinic doctrine of the Two Torahs—oral and written—both of which God revealed at Sinai.) God is the perfect interpreter, and the conceit of Jubilees is that it is the vessel of God's perfect interpretation.

The Word and the World

The terse and suggestive realism of the biblical narratives ultimately yielded to what we may call the figural interpretation of Scripture and the world. We have seen how this process began in the period after the public appearance of the Torah in the era of the return from the Babylonian Exile. A historical crisis and the appearance of a sacred text create fertile ground for the emergence of figural interpretation.

By figural interpretation I mean a way of reading in which the biblical text has a second level of meaning that pertains to another metaphysical or temporal order of reality, distinct from the reality of the here and now.[9] This "other" reality is accessible through the interpretation of the sacred text, and is often accompanied by ritual practices. Just as the biblical text comes to be seen, according to the four assumptions, as cryptic, relevant, perfect, and divine, so this "other" reality is cryptic, relevant, perfect, and divine.

This "other" reality is cryptic because it is hidden from the masses. The perception of it is available only to the enlightened few and their followers. It is relevant for the present, since one must reorder one's life in order to experience its power of transformation. It is a perfect reality in all respects. Finally, it is created by God. The cryptic, relevant, perfect, and divine world that figural interpretation reveals exists either in the near future, when God will utterly transform the material world, or in a spiritual plane that is beyond the material world. These two realities and their associated styles of figural interpretation—which I will call apocalyptic and Platonic (see the following chapters)—become dominant in Western culture for nearly two millennia, from roughly 300 BCE to 1600 CE, and in abridged form they persist in many circles until the present day. With the gift of figural interpretation, the Word becomes a secret window onto the hidden World, which holds salvation for those who can perceive it and who can change their lives according to its precepts.

The early interpretations of Genesis described above—from 1 Enoch, Jubilees, the Dead Sea Scrolls,

Philo, and rabbinic interpretation—deploy various features of figural interpretation. Enoch, Jubilees, and the Dead Sea Scrolls are primarily apocalyptic in their orientation toward Genesis and reality, while Philo is Platonic, and rabbinic interpretation is a complicated mixture of both.[10] In the next two chapters we will explore the character of apocalyptic and Platonic figural interpretations of Genesis, which flourished beginning in the Greco-Roman era.

Apocalyptic Secrets

"I know that such a person . . . was caught up into
Paradise and heard things that are not to be
told, that no mortal is permitted to repeat."

A New Creation

For over two thousand of years, the life of Genesis has been shaped by the belief that it is a repository of apocalyptic secrets, that is, revelations about the end of days, when the world will be remade. This is the oldest and most long-lived form of figural interpretation.

The word "apocalypse" is Greek for "uncovering" or "revelation." The central idea of apocalypticism is that God has granted a revelation about the imminent transformation of the world. Apocalypticism is a child of crisis. Not every crisis gives rise to apocalyptic ideas and expectations, but in the history of Judaism and Christianity, since the Babylonian conquest of Jerusalem in 586 BCE and the fifty years of Babylonian Exile that followed, nearly every crisis has yielded such responses.[1]

The crucial ingredient that made this crisis the dawn of apocalypticism was the availability and authority of sacred writings. This is the time when the book of Genesis and many other biblical books were crystallizing into final form. Apocalypticism has always been an intensely exegetical activity, calling for new interpretations from old authoritative texts. The Babylonian Exile was the first time that these two ingredients—crisis and textual exegesis—came together into a combustible mixture. During later centuries, particularly from the Greco-Roman age to early modernity, apocalyptic expectation was a dominant feature in most forms of Judaism and Christianity.

Apocalypticism is a way of providing hope at a time when hope seems futile. Time itself is disrupted, so that the evils of the present era will come to an end, and a once and future paradise will reappear. Since the future is, by definition, unknown, apocalypticism gives a way of filling the future with goodness and possibility, providing solace in the face of a bleak present. It is a way of allocating justice and reward in an unjust world, and it projects these longed-for realities into the near future. The Genesis stories of Creation and paradise provide crucial ingredients for the apocalyptic unveiling of the new Creation and the future paradise.

The River of Paradise

One of the key features of apocalypticism is the resurgence of mythic symbols and ideas. Let us look at one such symbol in Genesis—the rivers of paradise (Genesis 2:10–14). One of these four rivers is the Gihon, which "circles the land of Cush" (probably referring to Ethiopia). But the only river with this name elsewhere in the Bible is a small river in Jerusalem. The river Gihon in Genesis seems to suggest an association between the Garden of Eden and Jerusalem, and particularly the Jerusalem Temple. Like the Garden of Eden, the Temple is a place where humans are in the presence of God, and its interior is filled with images of sacred trees and cherubim. Not only are the doors and walls of the Temple carved with trees and cherubim, but two massive cherubim statues guard the Ark of the Covenant in the Temple's inner sanctum, corresponding to the cherubim in Eden who "guard the way to the Tree of Life" (Genesis 3:24). The Eden symbolism of the Temple suggests, as Jon Levenson writes, "that the Temple was, in fact, a paradise."[2]

In Ezekiel 40–48, written during the crisis of the Babylonian Exile, an angel reveals to the prophet an apocalyptic vision of the future Temple. The vision reaches a climax when the angel leads him to the east side of the Temple, where the river Gihon—the river of paradise—flows.

> He said to me, "Do you see, O son of man?" And he led me back to the bank of the river. As I came back, behold, on the bank of the river there were a great many trees on one side and the other. And he said to me, "These waters flow toward the eastern region and descend to the wilderness. And when they come to the sea—the Sea of Bitterness—the waters will heal." (Ezekiel 47:6–8)

The Sea of Bitterness is the Dead Sea, a pool of lifeless water. At the end of days the river of paradise will heal these waters, and they will teem with life:

> Every living creature that swarms will live wherever the river flows, and there will be a great many fish when these waters come there. (Ezekiel 47:9).

This description of the birth of new life in the Dead Sea echoes the description of God's creation of sea life in Genesis 1: "God said, 'Let the waters swarm with swarms of living creatures'" (Genesis 1:20). The verse in Ezekiel—"every living creature that swarms will live"— alludes to this act of creation. The new era of life and abundance will be a return to the perfect world at the time of creation, when it was unsullied by sin, violence, and corruption.

Ezekiel's vision concludes with a panorama of miraculous trees growing on the banks of the river:

> Along the river will grow, on its banks on one side and the other, every kind of tree for food. Their leaves will not wither, nor will their fruit fail. They will yield new fruit every month. (Ezekiel 47:12)

The ever-abundant fruit of the miraculous trees recalls the trees that God planted in the Garden of Eden: "[He] caused to grow from the soil every tree pleasant to the sight and good for food" (Genesis 2:9). These trees provided Adam and Eve with abundant fruit for as long as they lived in the Garden. The future paradise will be a new Garden of Eden, where the bitter waters are healed and humans can live a perfect life.

The refashioning of Genesis in this apocalyptic text sets the tone for later apocalyptic visions and interpretations. The idyllic existence of primeval times becomes the idyllic existence of the future times—the beginning-time returns in the end-time. This is one of the first apocalyptic texts, and in it the beginnings in Genesis become a model and a promise for the perfect future.

The End of Days

The idea that Genesis contains revelations of divine secrets about the end of days is a product not only of apocalyptic beliefs but also of intensely close readings of Genesis. If, as we discussed previously, the biblical writings came to be seen in postexilic times as cryptic, relevant, perfect, and divine, then every detail of the text must be examined closely to uncover its deeper meaning. Intensely close readings are characteristic of apocalyptic interpretation: the apocalyptic reader is always searching for clues that point to the text's apocalyptic secrets, its cryptic and perfect meanings.

One clue that Genesis contains secrets about the end of days is found at the beginning of "The Blessing of Jacob" in Genesis 49. In this chapter, Jacob on his deathbed seems to turn into a prophet, telling his sons what will happen to their descendants: "Jacob called to his sons, saying, 'Gather, so that I may tell you what will happen to you in the days to come'" (Genesis 49:1). The prophetic quality of this scene is obvious, and like a real prophet Jacob now begins to speak in poetry. But to an apocalyptic reader, the future that Jacob addresses has a more specific nature. The Hebrew phrase *'aharit hayyamim* means "the days to come," or more idiomatically, "the future." For the apocalyptic interpreter, however, the words contain a secret held by their literal translation, "the end of days"—Jacob is really speaking about the end-time when God will transform the world. The hyper-literal meaning of the words replaces their idiomatic meaning, and Jacob now becomes an apocalyptic seer, revealing his vision of the end-time.

We have seen previously how Jacob's blessing of Judah becomes the seed for the idea of a messiah from the line of David. When Jacob prophesies, "The scepter shall not depart from Judah" (Genesis 49:10), he utters an apocalyptic secret. As we saw above, this prophecy is deciphered in the Dead Sea Scrolls:

> The scepter shall [n]ot depart from the tribe of Judah. . . . Until the messiah of righteousness comes, the branch of David. For the covenant of his people's kingship has been given to him and his descendants for everlasting generations. (*Commentary on Genesis* A [4Q252])

Since Jacob is speaking about "the end of days," the idea of a messiah who will have an everlasting rule in the future idyllic era makes perfect sense. The apocalyptic reading derives from a close reading of the literal—but not the idiomatic—sense of Jacob's blessing. It is a mix of apocalyptic longing for a perfect world and hyper-close attention to the clues in the text.

The Palestinian Targums, which are a marvelous blend of interpretation and translation (into Aramaic), make this apocalyptic reading of "The Blessing of Jacob" abundantly clear. Here is the rendering of Genesis 49:1 from the earliest of these Targums:

And Jacob called his sons and said to them,
"Gather together and I will tell you the concealed
secrets, the hidden ends, the giving of the rewards
of the just, and the punishment of the wicked, and
what the happiness of Eden is." (*Targum Neofiti*, at
Genesis 49:1)[3]

In this rendering, Jacob is now a full-blown apocalyptic seer, and his blessings are a revelation of all the secrets of the end-days. Genesis has become a book of apocalyptic secrets.

The Glory of Adam

In the apocalyptic circles of the postexilic era, the secrets of Genesis were not just good to think about, but also good to live by. The revelations of divine secrets changed people's understandings of reality and, for the deeply committed, led to new ways of life. The first full-blown apocalyptic community that we know about is the community of the Dead Sea Scrolls, who lived near the barren shores of the Dead Sea from the second century BCE to the first century CE.[4] These people refashioned their lives according to the apocalyptic secrets they gleaned from Genesis and other sacred writings.

Members of this community—probably a group called the Essenes (Greek *Essaioi*) or "Pious Ones" (Aramaic *ḥassaya*)—retreated from civilization to purify themselves in the desert. They did this to fulfill the prophecy of Isaiah:

> A voice calls out:
> Prepare in the desert the way of Yahweh,
> Make straight in the wilderness a road for our God.
> (Isaiah 40:3)

They took this verse as an apocalyptic command to prepare for the end-time. But where in the desert should they go? Which is the right wilderness to prepare the way of the Lord? Isaiah doesn't give enough directions to locate the place for a new apocalyptic community.

The founders of the Dead Sea Scroll group combined the Isaiah passage with the geography of Ezekiel's vision of the river of paradise. As Ezekiel foretells, the region of the Dead Sea, which was now a lifeless desert, will in the end-time become a lush and miraculously fruitful place. Its waters will be healed, and the desert will return to the glory of paradise. The site of Qumran, near the northwest shore of the Dead Sea, is approximately where the river of paradise will flow into the Dead Sea. The desert community is the future location of Paradise Central, a new Garden of Eden.

The people of Qumran were ascetics, living a harsh and simple life in the wilderness. But their asceticism was, paradoxically, a foretaste of their future life in the restored Garden of Eden. They believed themselves to be living "in the company of angels," alongside holy divine beings. This is probably why they were celibate—

since angels don't have sex (see, similarly, Mark 12:25)—and this is probably why they wore white linen robes, which are the garments of angels (see Daniel 10:5, 12:6–7). This is probably also why they took purifying baths whenever they entered their settlement, since they had to be pure and holy like the angels. It was a life of purity and perfection, a taste of paradise in the present, while they prepared the way of the Lord and waited expectantly for their exaltation at the end of days.

The way they would be exalted brings us back to their apocalyptic reading of Genesis. At the end of days, according to the community's texts, they will regain "all the glory of Adam." This phrase, *kol kevod 'adam*, occurs several times in the community's texts, and refers to the glorious existence that the community's members will experience when God intervenes in this wicked age to change the world completely. The two main rule-books of the community describe how God will bestow "all the glory of Adam" upon them in the final days:

> These are the spiritual foundations for the Sons of Truth in the world. The reward of all those who walk in it will be healing, plentiful peace in a long life, fruitful offspring with all everlasting blessings, eternal joy with endless life, and a crown of glory with majestic robes in eternal light. . . . God has chosen them for an everlasting covenant and to them shall belong all the glory of Adam. (*Rule of the Community* [1QS] iv.6–7, 22–23)[5]

God, in his wonderful mysteries, atoned for their iniquity and pardoned their sin. And he built for them a safe home in Israel, such as there has not been since ancient times, not until now. Those who remained steadfast in it will acquire eternal life, and all the glory of Adam is for them. (*Damascus Document* [CD-A] iii.18–20)[6]

For "the Sons of Truth" who "remain steadfast" in their "safe home in Israel," the reward of the end-time will be a return to the existence that Adam once had in the Garden of Eden. There will be no death, but rather "eternal life." There will be no sorrow, but rather "eternal joy with endless life." There will be no curses of painful labor and childbirth, but rather "fruitful offspring with all everlasting blessings." There will be no violence, but rather "plentiful peace in a long life." Just as the river of paradise heals the Dead Sea, "the reward of all those who walk in [truth] will be healing."

The clothing that these people will wear in the new Eden suggests a change to nearly divine status, as if they will become "like gods" (Genesis 3:4, 22) in paradise. They will wear "a crown of glory with majestic robes in eternal light." This image of shining garments recalls the description of God in the book of Psalms:

You are clothed in majesty and grandeur,
Wrapped in light like a robe.

(Psalm 104:1–2)

But the "Sons of Truth in the world" will not be wearing God's clothing, they will be wearing Adam's. This wardrobe belongs to "all the glory of Adam." The shining robes indicate his exalted status in the Garden of Eden before his transgression and expulsion. This is the perfect life that the Qumran community expected to come upon them on the day of the great transformation. On that day, according to one of their fragmentary texts,

> there will be no more guilty deeds on the earth and not [. . . destr]oyer, and every adversary. And all the world will be like Eden, and all [. . .] the earth will be at peace forever. (*Renewed Earth* [4Q475])[7]

The whole world will be "like Eden," there will be "peace forever," and there will be no more "guilty deeds." This is a life in paradise, but this time with no "adversary," no *maśṭem*, a word that calls to mind the arch-adversary, named Mastema, Belial, or Satan. In the new earth, there will be only goodness and blessings, abundant joy, and garments of light. This is a return to the perfect life that Adam and Eve lost, but it will be restored to the faithful at the end of time. God will forgive their sins, and he will exalt them with Adam's glory:

> You have raised an [eternal] name, [forgiving] offense, casting away all their iniquities, giving them as a legacy all the glory of Adam [and] abundance of days. (*Hodayot* [1QH^a] iv.15)[8]

As it happened, the Essenes did not survive the brutal retaliation of the Roman army during the Great Revolt against Rome (68–70 CE). Qumran became a ruin, and the community's scrolls were hidden away in nearby caves, only to be discovered some fifty years ago. Their apocalyptic dreams became food for worms, surviving in tattered bits of parchment and papyrus. But the pious expectation to shine one day with the glory of Adam persisted in a nearby apocalyptic community, the early Christians.

The Last Adam

The letters of Paul are the earliest Christian texts, written in the 50's CE, contemporary with the Essene community at Qumran. There is no reason to think that Paul was directly influenced by the Essenes or their doctrines; their common features can be taken to suggest a heritage of shared religious concepts among all Jewish groups of the time. Paul, like most other Jews, avidly expected the end-time to arrive soon. After his conversion on the road to Damascus (Acts 9), Paul became a Christian and an apostle to the Gentiles.

In his second letter to the Christian community at Corinth, Paul describes a "vision and revelation" that "a person" had fourteen years previously. He is probably describing his own conversion:

> I will go on to visions and revelations of the Lord. I know a person in Christ who fourteen years ago

was caught up to the third heaven—whether in the body or out of the body I do not know; God knows. And I know that such a person—whether in the body or out of the body I do not know; God knows—was caught up into Paradise and heard things that are not to be told, that no mortal is permitted to repeat. (2 Corinthians 12:14)[9]

This is Paul's "vision and revelation" of divine mysteries. It is his apocalyptic vision, which transformed him into a Christian apostle. This is a visionary ascent to the celestial Garden of Eden, in the third heaven, where divine knowledge is revealed to the holy seer. Paul does not tell us what he heard in the heavenly paradise, for such things are divine secrets "that no mortal is permitted to repeat." And yet these apocalyptic secrets became the core of his Christian faith and his knowledge of what will come at the end of days.

Paul's apocalyptic knowledge draws on the idea of Adam's primeval glory, which we know from Qumran, but Paul now sees that it will be restored to humanity through Christ.[10] Since he understands Adam as "the pattern of the one who was to come" (Romans 5:14), it is Christ, not Adam, who now bears God's glory. We can see this conceptual shift in the following texts, from Qumran and from the New Testament:

[Adam], our [fa]ther, you fashioned in the image of [your] glory. (*Words of the Luminaries*[a] [4Q504] viii.4)[11]

CHAPTER 3

> "[Christ] is the reflection of God's glory and the
> exact imprint of God's very being." (Hebrews 1:3)

In the New Testament, Adam's glory becomes Christ's glory. Through Christ, the righteous will slough off the material body and take on a spiritual body, "conformed to the image of His Son" (Romans 8:29). Then they will ascend at last to heaven, perhaps to the celestial Garden of Eden, where Paul ascended briefly during his lifetime and learned the heavenly secrets.

In his first letter to the Corinthians, Paul tells how this mysterious transformation will take place:

> Listen, I will tell you a mystery! We will not all die,
> but we will all be changed, in a moment, in the
> twinkling of an eye, at the last trumpet. For the
> trumpet will sound, and the dead will be raised im-
> perishable, and we will be changed. For this perish-
> able body must put on imperishability, and this
> mortal body must put on immortality. (1 Corinthi-
> ans 15:51–53)

This change from a mortal body to an imperishable and immortal body is similar to the future apocalyptic transformation of "the Sons of Truth" in the Qumran texts. But now the Christian in the end-time will take on the imperishable and immortal body of Christ, the new Adam.

The glory of Christ, like the glory of Adam, is a reflection of the glory of God, in whose image Adam and Christ were created. Paul describes the future transformation of the Christian body in terms of the contrast between Adam's physical body and Christ's spiritual body:

> The first man, Adam, became a living being; the last Adam became a life-giving spirit. But it is not the spiritual that is first, but the physical, and then the spiritual. The first man was from the earth, a man of dust; the second man is from heaven. As was the man of dust, so are those who are of the dust; and as is the man of heaven, so are those who are of heaven. Just as we have borne the image of the man of dust, we will also bear the image of the man of heaven. (1 Corinthians 15:45–49)

In other words, we all begin like the first man, Adam, with a body of dust—a physical and mortal body. But at the end of days, those in Christ will "bear the image of the man of heaven," that is, a spiritual body. For Paul, the great mystery will occur when the physical body, which we inherit from "the first man," is transformed into "the image of the man of heaven." The transformation into Christ's glorious spiritual body is the ultimate reward.

At the end of days, not only will the Children of God obtain the glory of a spiritual body, but nature as a whole will share the same glory:

> Creation itself will be set free from the bondage of decay and will obtain the freedom of the glory of the children of God. (Romans 8:21)

In other words, the world will become a paradise, where God's glory—through Christ—will transform a fallen world into a new and perfect creation. This divine glory will change humanity and the world into spiritual glory "in the twinkling of an eye, at the last trumpet."

Like the people of Qumran, Paul expected this mysterious change to occur during his lifetime. In his earliest letter he writes, "We who are alive, who are left, will be caught up in the clouds together with [the resurrected dead] to meet the Lord in the air; and so we will be with the Lord forever" (1 Thessalonians 17). However, like the men of Qumran, Paul died before the great transformation at the end of days. Much time has passed since then, and a lot has changed, but many Christians still await the moment when the last trumpet will sound, and they will ascend, transformed into the glory of the Last Adam.

Apocalyptic Dualism

Our examples from Ezekiel, the Dead Sea Scrolls, and the New Testament show us how Genesis came to be seen as a book of apocalyptic secrets. The combination of crisis and intensive interpretation of Holy Scripture yielded a way of reading that unlocked scriptural secrets about the end-time. The Garden of Eden, the rivers of paradise, Jacob's blessings about "the end of days," the blessed life of Adam before his transgression—all of these were viewed as mysteries that reveal to the faithful interpreter God's plan for the glorious future.

The Essenes and Paul saw the world of their own time as being under the authority of evil powers—for the Essenes, Belial and the malign powers of darkness, and for Paul, the evil forces that he calls "rulers," "authorities," and "cosmic powers." Paul writes:

> Our struggle is not against enemies of blood and flesh, but against the rulers, against the authorities, against the cosmic powers of this present darkness, against the spiritual forces of evil in the heavenly places. (Ephesians 6:12)

The Dead Sea Scrolls similarly describe the legacy of these evil forces:

> From the Angel of Darkness stems the corruption of all the Sons of Justice, and all their sins, their iniquities, their guilts and their offensive deeds are under his dominion in compliance with the mysteries of God, until his moment. And all their afflictions and their periods of grief are caused by the dominion of his enmity. And all the spirits of his lot cause the Sons of Light to fall. (*Rule of the Community* [1QS] iii.2024)[12]

The evil cosmic forces of "this present darkness" are in command "in compliance with the mysteries of God." But their rule will come to an end at the great transformation at the end of days, when God and the angels of Light will prevail over the demonic spirits. The evil of this world-age will come to an end, and a new perfect era will dawn, a new paradise.

The worldview of apocalypticism is dualistic. The focus is on the two cosmic forces—of good and evil, light and darkness—and two periods of time in which they rule. The corrupt world-age in which we live is under the rule of darkness and evil powers. The perfect world-to-come will be under the rule of God and the powers of eternal goodness. For the Essenes, the Children of Light will be exalted; for Paul, the Children of God. The chosen people—Essenes or Christians, depending on the source—will dwell like angels in paradise, like Adam, who was created to dwell in paradise. Life in Eden will be restored, and the redeemed will live like Adam or like the Last Adam.

These apocalyptic communities saw themselves as dwelling on the boundary between two ages. Their "now" was the last days of "this present darkness," and they already tasted the angelic and perfect life to come. They anticipated that the end of days would come soon, during their lifetime, and they would dwell in goodness and blessing forever. Their existence was perched between "now" and "to-come," in the twilight between darkness and light. For the apocalyptic believer, the present is slowly fading, and the future is almost in sight.

The dualistic view of reality in apocalypticism has a counterpart in its dualistic view of Scripture. Genesis tells of things that happened in the past, but its secret apocalyptic senses are revelations about the future.

Like reality itself, the words of Genesis have two faces, one looking backward into the formative past and one looking forward into the redemptive future. The Garden of Eden, the rivers of paradise, the glory of Adam, and all the other details in Genesis have dual reference, one regarding the past, which is plain to anyone who reads it, and one concerning the mysteries of the future, which is only available to apocalyptic seers and interpreters.

A Dead Sea Scroll says this about the Essene master, the Teacher of Righteousness: "God made known to him all the mysteries of the words of his servants, the prophets."[13] The prophet Moses was believed to have written Genesis, but the secrets of Genesis were revealed later, to the Teacher of Righteousness, to Jesus, to Paul, and to the many other apocalyptic interpreters in the years since.

In the revelations of apocalypticism, Genesis becomes a two-layered book, with public and secret senses, just as the world becomes a two-layered structure, consisting of this world and the world-to-come. This world is like the dust of Adam's body, like the plain words of Genesis, and will soon fade away. The coming era is like Adam's glory, like the apocalyptic secrets of Genesis, like the scent of paradise. Now, as Paul says, we read Genesis "through a glass darkly," but its secrets will become crystal clear at the end of days, when its mysteries are fulfilled.

Platonic Worlds

"When soaring upward the mind . . . is carried around with the dances of the planets and fixed stars, in accordance with the laws of perfect music, following the love of wisdom that guides it."

Out of the Cave

Alfred North Whitehead famously wrote that all of Western philosophy is "a series of footnotes to Plato."[1] What is at least as true, if less obvious, is that all of Western religion also owes a deep debt to Plato. Throughout much of its life, Genesis has been filtered and shaped by Platonic ideas. Beginning with the conquests of Alexander the Great, Judaism became deeply imbued with Greek ways of thought and practice, creating a synthesis that continued in Judaism and in its daughter religion, Christianity, for well over a thousand years. For the Platonist, the Bible and the world are seen as part of a dual reality, which consists of visible and invisible things. The visible, material world is the realm of imperfection and change, where individuals are born, live, and die. The invisible, higher world is the realm of perfect being, where the true forms of things exist eternally. The hidden senses of Genesis provide a path to this ideal world, liberating us from bondage to the material world.

The roots of the Platonic Genesis are in book 7 of *The Republic*, where Plato relates his famous allegory of the cave. The cave is a symbol of this world, the world of the senses. What we see in this world are only the shadows of things, not things as they truly are. Only the philosopher can ascend out of the cave and see things truly in the upper world. Plato explains the meaning of this allegorical story:

> The upward journey and the sight of things up on
> the surface of the earth [are] the mind's ascent to
> the intelligible realm. . . . The last thing to be
> seen—and it isn't easy to see—in the intelligible
> realm is the idea of the good; and the sight of it
> leads one to deduce that it is responsible for every-
> thing that is right and beautiful. (*Republic*
> 517b–c)[2]

The "intelligible realm" is the world of ideal forms, which only the intellect can perceive. This is the invisible world of "being," which is perfect and unchanging, in contrast to the material world, which is the realm of "becoming," where things are imperfect and transient. The goal of the philosopher, according to Plato, is to make an intellectual ascent to the intelligible world, to see things as they truly are, and then return to this world and instruct others—or in the case of the philosopher-king, to rule them.

In Plato's philosophy, reality is dualistic. The world of everyday life—the material world—is a flawed copy of the world of ideal forms. This everyday world is dominated by beliefs, emotions, and prejudices, not by true knowledge. Our senses are attuned to this shadow-world, so we assume it to be the only world. Only the philosophical mind can overrule the senses and see the invisible, timeless, and perfect world that exists outside of the cave. This is Plato's call to his followers—to seek the real and the good, which exist in pure form beyond the limits of the material world.

The philosophical idea that pure forms exist beyond the material world derives in part from the logic of mathematics and geometry, as developed by Pythagoras and his school. Pythagoras's theorem, which we all remember vaguely from high school, has to do with a right-angled triangle: $a^2 + b^2 = c^2$ (the sum of the squared lengths of the right-angle sides equals the squared length of the hypotenuse). But the theorem does not apply to any particular instance of a triangle that a person might see or draw, which is inevitably crooked and imperfect. It has to do with the idea of a perfect triangle with perfect angles. Such "true" triangles don't exist in the material world. Therefore mathematics and geometry must refer to an ideal world, a world where perfect triangles, squares, and tetrahedrons truly exist.

Plato took this model of the ideal world of math and geometry and drew the inference that ideal forms exist for all things in this world. A particular bed is merely an imperfect instantiation of the ideal form of "bed," and so on for everything else. In the *Republic*, Plato generally illustrates the ideal forms by using ethical qualities, like "justice" and "beauty," rather than artifacts and natural substances like a human being or a rose. The transcendent form of "the good," according to Plato, is the source not only of all value but also of all reality. This ideal form is Plato's non-anthropomorphic concept of divinity.

Plato applied his distinction between ideal forms and imperfect physical copies to the creation of the cosmos in his dialogue *Timaeus*. This is a dense and difficult work, which is presented not as the truth, but as a myth or "plausible story." In it Plato details how the material world was created by a divine craftsman after the plan of the ideal world. He also argues that mathematical relationships underlie all the structures of the cosmos. The *Timaeus* was the most influential of all of Plato's works until the rise of modern scientific cosmology in the seventeenth century. Although the details of the work were superseded, Galileo and Newton demonstrated that mathematics really does explain the structure of the cosmos.

Plato's cosmology anticipates modern science in its reliance on mathematics, but it also has features that are curiously similar to some of the Creation accounts in the Bible. According to the *Timaeus*, a divine "craftsman" (*demiourgos*) consulted the ideal world as a blueprint for the material world. This is reminiscent of God's reliance on a semi-personified Wisdom (*hokmah*) as his "craftsman" (*'amon*) when he created the cosmos, according to Proverbs 8. Plato's primal craftsman then formed the material world out of a preexisting substance that was "invisible" (*anoratos*) and "formless" (*amorphos*; *Timaeus* 51a). This is reminiscent of the preexisting "formless chaos" (*tohu wa-bohu*) in Genesis 1:2. Plato's craftsman "brought it from a state of disorder to one of order, because he believed that order was in every way better than disorder" (*Timaeus* 30a). This is similar to God's pronouncement that the newly created universe was "very good" (Genesis 1:31).

These similarities made it easy to assimilate Plato's teachings to the model of Creation in Genesis.

The Platonic craftsman made the world to be good, but he was limited by the defects of its physical nature: "He wanted to produce a piece of work that would be as excellent and supreme as its nature would allow" (*Timaeus* 30b). Perfect goodness only exists in the ideal world, of which our world is only a shadow. The duality of the material and ideal world explains why our everyday world is imperfect, and it provides a path for seeking the higher, perfect world. Plato's cosmology, with various revisions, came to dominate much of Greek philosophy. When the Jews entered the Greek world, it was only natural for them to blend Plato's cosmology with Genesis.

The Greek Genesis

In 333 BCE Alexander the Great defeated Darius, king of the Persian Empire. This year (which is delightfully easy to remember) began a new era in ancient history and brought the Jews into the Greek world.[3] Sometime during the third century BCE, the Pentateuch was translated into Greek. This translation project took place in the city of Alexandria, a great center of learning and the new capital city of Egypt under Alexander's successors. Alexandria had a large Greek-speaking Jewish community, and so it was a natural place for the creation of the Greek Genesis. This translation of the

Pentateuch came to be called the Septuagint ("Seventy") because of a later legend that seventy-two Jewish scholars made independent translations over a period of seventy-two days, and when they compared them, the translations were identical to the letter! This legend emphasizes God's approval of the translation. As Philo of Alexandria, a Jewish sage of the first century CE, commented:

> [We] designate the authors not as translators but as prophets and interpreters of sacred mysteries, to whom it was granted in the purity of their thought to match their steps with the purest of spirits, the spirit of Moses. (*Life of Moses* 40)[4]

The Greek Genesis is, for the most part, a careful word-by-word translation.[5] Yet though it is faithful to the Hebrew, the Greek words sometimes betray the Platonic philosophical ideas of the translators. The translators were learned scholars, well-educated Hellenistic Jews, whose worldview blended biblical and Greek ideas together in varying measures. In their choice of translation equivalents we sometimes get a taste of how Genesis became Platonic.

As we have seen, the picture of the preexisting substance in Genesis and the *Timaeus* is startlingly similar. According to Genesis 1:2, "the earth was *tohu wabohu*," which the King James Version translates as "unformed and void." The Hebrew phrase is difficult to translate—*tohu* means "wasteland" or "chaos," and *bohu* doesn't mean anything—it's a nonsense word that rhymes with *tohu*. The Septuagint translators gave a careful word-by-word rendering: "the earth was unseen and unorganized." Why did they use these words —"unseen" (*aoratos*) and "unorganized" (*akataskeuastos*)—to translate *tohu wa-bohu*? The answer is found in the *Timaeus*, where the preexisting substance was "invisible" (*anoratos*) and "formless" (*amorphos*). The translators used familiar Platonic language for the preexisting substance in Genesis. In other words, to these translators, Plato and Moses were saying the same thing. Here we see how the Greek Genesis blends together Greek and Hebrew concepts.

The Platonic flavor of Creation in the Greek Genesis does not mean that it is a bad translation, but simply that it is a translation. All translations mingle the concepts and categories of the source language with those of the target language. The words and the ideas of Genesis take on Greek color because they are now written in Greek. The Septuagint became the standard Scripture for Greek-speaking Jews and for most Christians, including all the writers of the New Testament. And this means that Genesis described, for them and their descendants, a Platonic world.

The Ascent of the Soul

Philo of Alexandria, a contemporary of Jesus and Paul, fully synthesized the worlds of Judaism and Greek philosophy in his commentaries on Genesis and Exodus.

In his writings Plato and Moses speak in harmony. Harry Wolfson called Philo the inventor of philosophical religion, a style of thought and practice that dominated Judaism and Christianity until the early modern era, and that still influences our contemporary religious ideas.[6] Even though Philo is largely forgotten today, his legacy—philosophical religion over the ages—still looms large.

Philo consolidated the efforts of his predecessors (mostly Alexandrian Jews) in reading the Bible through the lens of Greek philosophy. In part he wanted to show that Jewish thought is every bit as sophisticated as Greek, and that Moses anticipated Plato's philosophy. Philo's voluminous commentaries blend Greek ideas with the four assumptions of early biblical interpreters—that the Bible is cryptic, relevant, perfect, and divine. But in its cryptic senses he found not apocalyptic secrets but philosophical wisdom.

For Philo, the Bible was a dualistic text, whose sensible meanings were but the shadow of its eternal and perfect meanings. He wrote, "the contents of the Law [are] visible symbols of things invisible, expressing the inexpressible."[7] In the spirit of Plato's allegory of the cave, Philo described the method of uncovering the hidden philosophical senses as "allegorical interpretation":

> Go forward in quest of the allegorical interpretation, in the conviction that the words of the [bibli-

cal] oracles are, as it were, shadows cast by bodies, whereas the significations therein revealed are the things that have true existence. (*Confusion of Tongues* 190)[8]

The words of the Bible are like "shadows," an allusion to Plato's allegory of the cave. Their deeper meanings concern "things that have true existence," referring to the upper world of pure forms outside of the cave. Philo made the allegory of the cave into a method of biblical interpretation. The words of Genesis are shadows and symbols of higher things. Their true meanings reveal the light that shines beyond the shadows, the "things invisible" that have "true existence." Genesis and reality each have two dimensions, the lesser one perceived by the senses and the greater one perceived by the philosophical mind.

This method allows Philo to solve many problems in Genesis. For example, consider the apparent contradiction of God's twofold creation of Adam:

God created man in his image; in God's image he created him; male and female he created them. (Genesis 1:27)

God Yahweh formed a man from the soil's dust. He blew life's breath into his nostrils, and the man became a living creature. (Genesis 2:7)

We have seen (chapter 1) that this repetition is the result of the editorial combination of the P and J Creation accounts. But this explanation was not available to Philo and would have been inconceivable to him anyway, since he believed that God revealed the words of Genesis to Moses at Mount Sinai. To solve the problem of this doubled creation, Philo pursued the hidden philosophical sense, guided by hints in the text.

To a good Platonist, the solution is clear.[9] The first creation of Adam occurs in the intelligible world of ideal forms. Notice that God creates Adam "in God's image," which must refer to the invisible world, since God is invisible and therefore his "image" must be an ideal form. The first creation of Adam, Philo concludes, refers to the ideal form of Adam. The second creation obviously occurs in the material world, since God fashions Adam "from the soil's dust" and Adam becomes "a living creature." The ideal Adam exists only in the upper, intelligible world, of which the physical Adam is an earthly copy. As Philo explains:

> [Moses] shows very clearly that there is an immense difference between the man now fashioned and the one created earlier after the image of God. For the molded man is sense-perceptible, partaking already of specific quality, framed of body and soul, man or woman, by nature mortal; whereas he that was after the image was an idea or genus or seal, intelligible, incorporeal, neither male nor female, imperishable by nature. (*Creation of the World* 134)[10]

This is a persuasive explanation of the two creations of Adam, as long as one believes in the twofold Platonic world.

For Philo, as for Plato, the highest calling is the wise man's philosophical ascent from the cave of this world. The "visible symbols" of this philosophical and spiritual quest are the call and migration of the patriarch Abraham. God says to Abraham: "Go forth from your land, from your kindred, and from your father's house to the land that I will show you. I will make you into a great nation, and I will bless you" (Genesis 12:1). Philo elucidates the hidden philosophical sense of these words:

> Intent on purifying man's soul, God initially assigns as its starting point for full salvation its migration out of three regions: body, sense perception, and speech. "Land" is a symbol of body, "kindred" of sense perception, "father's house" of speech. . . . Go forth, then, from the earthly matter that envelops you. Escape, man, from the abominable prison, your body, and from the pleasures and lusts that act as its jailers. (*Migration of Abraham* 2, 9)[11]

The goal—for the Abraham and for the soul—is the ascent to true wisdom, to "being" rather than "becoming." At times Philo waxes lyrical about this ascent, describing it as a mystical journey to the higher Platonic world:

> When soaring upward the mind . . . is carried around with the dances of the planets and fixed stars, in accordance with the laws of perfect music,

following the love of wisdom that guides it. When it has transcended all sensible substance, at that point it longs for the intelligible, and on beholding in that realm beauties beyond measure, the patterns and original of the sensible things in the world below, it is possessed by a sober intoxication like those seized with wild frenzy, and is inspired. . . . Escorted by this to the uppermost vault of things intelligible, it seems to be on its way to the Great King himself; but while it keenly strives to see him, pure and untempered rays of concentrated light stream forth like a flood, so that through its flashing bursts, the eye of the understanding spins. (*Creation of the World*, 70–71)[12]

The philosophical ascent of the intellect seems to merge with the mystical experience of the seer who ascends to the presence of God. The invisible, eternal world of pure forms becomes a vision of heaven and a revelation of God's inconceivable mystery. In Philo's spiritual journey, Plato joins forces with Moses and the biblical prophets in the upward ascent to God and true blessedness.

Jerusalem Above and Below

Another sage who ascended to heavenly mysteries in the upper world was Paul (see above, chapter 3). His was a Platonic ascent to the invisible world *and* an initiation into apocalyptic secrets. Paul, an educated Hellenistic Jew, shows his affinity for Platonic language and concepts throughout his writings. For instance, in his letter to the Christian community in Rome, he writes about the knowledge of God among the Gentiles:

> What is known of God is manifest among them, for God has manifested it to them. For since the creation of the cosmos, God's invisible qualities—his eternal power and divine nature—have been clearly seen from what has been created. (Romans 1:19–20)

This is Platonic language about knowledge of the invisible and visible worlds: the realm of "God's invisible qualities" and the visible realm of "what has been created."

Paul also appeals to these two worlds in his interpretation of Genesis. He comments in Platonic fashion on Abraham's two wives, Sarah and Hagar. Like Philo, he describes the hidden sense of Genesis as an allegory.

> Now this is an allegory: these women are two covenants. One woman, in fact, is Hagar, from Mount Sinai, bearing children for slavery. Now Hagar . . . corresponds to the present Jerusalem, for she is in slavery with her children. But the other woman corresponds to the Jerusalem above; she is free, and she is our mother. (Galatians 4:24–26)

Paul sees the dualism of Sarah and Hagar as biblical symbols of the "Jerusalem above" and "the present Jerusalem," that is, the Jerusalem below. The heavenly Jerusalem is "our mother"—she is the perfect origin of Paul's Christian followers, who are symbolically represented by the chosen son, Isaac. The earthly Jerusalem, which is "from Mount Sinai," where God gave the Law, enslaves her children to the Law. These slave children—symbolically represented by Ishmael—are the Jews, who are obliged to keep the Law, and may also include those Christians who keep the Law. The latter are followers of Paul's rivals, James and Peter, who live in "the present Jerusalem" (see Galatians 1:18–2:14).

In his allegorical interpretation of Genesis, Paul's contrasts of Law versus Faith and Slavery versus Freedom are organized according to the Platonic worlds of the Jerusalem above and the Jerusalem below. The former is perfect and spiritually fruitful, mother to the true faith, while the latter is earthly, corrupt, and enslaved to the Law. This is not an apocalyptic New Jerusalem, which will descend from heaven at the end-time (as in Revelation 21), but a Platonic Jerusalem, the pure and invisible form of which the earthly Jerusalem is an imperfect and flawed copy—an earthly shadow that yields false knowledge and false religion.

We have seen previously that Paul is an apocalyptic interpreter of Genesis, reading its hidden meanings as oriented toward salvation in the end-time. Now we see that he is also a Platonic interpreter, reading the secret sense of Genesis as oriented toward the relationship between the redemptive truth of the invisible world above—which exists beyond time and change—and the burden of slavery in the world below.

The Gnostic Genesis

The strangest blend of Plato and Genesis is found in the sacred texts of Christian Gnosticism, a loosely organized movement popular in the second to fourth centuries CE, until it was suppressed as a heresy.[13] The most important Gnostic interpretation of Genesis is *The Secret Revelation of John*. This is one of the famous Gnostic Gospels discovered in the Egyptian desert in 1945. As Karen King writes, *The Secret Revelation of John* is "the first Christian writing to formulate a comprehensive narrative of the nature of God, the origin of the world, and human salvation."[14] And it does it through a Platonizing reimagining of Genesis.

According to this Gnostic Genesis, the material world and the ideal world are moral opposites. The material world was created by an evil God who could not perceive the ideal world above him. The evil creator is named Yaldabaoth, which means, roughly, "Child (of) Chaos," alluding to the chaos (*bohu*) of Genesis 1:2. He is also called Saklas ("Fool") and Samael, one of the names of Satan:

Now this weak ruler has three names. The first is Yaldabaoth. The second is Saklas. The third is Samael. He is impious in his madness. . . . For he said,

"I am God and no other god exists except me,"
since he is ignorant of the place from which his
strength had come. (*Secret Revelation of John*
12.7–13)

In this passage Yaldabaoth paraphrases the First Commandment: "I am Yahweh your God; you shall have no
other gods beside me." In other words, Yaldabaoth is
the God of the Bible, but in the Gnostic revision he is
a weak and deceived God, since he does not know the
perfect God.

The luminous and perfect God is in the world
above, a Platonic world of pure understanding. The
high God creates three perfect beings in the upper
world—Wisdom, the Self-Created Christ, and the Perfect Human, Adam:

> From the first Understanding and the perfect
> Mind, through God. . . . It named the true Perfect
> Human, the primal revelation, Adam. It set him
> over the primal realm beside the great divine Self-
> Created Christ. . . . And the invisible Spirit gave
> him an unconquerable intellectual power. (*Secret
> Revelation of John* 9.1–4)

This is the Gnostic interpretation of God's creation of
the first man "in the image of God" in Genesis 1:27.

In the world below, Yaldabaoth creates the lower
Adam, who is fashioned after a reflection of the high
God ("the holy and perfect Mother-Father") in the pri-
meval waters. But Yaldabaoth and his fellow gods grow

jealous of Adam, because he is wiser than they, and they cast him into the material world. This is the Gnostic version of the creation of Adam in Genesis. Then the high God above has mercy on Adam, and sends him "luminous Thought," who is the ideal form of Eve. She will teach him the knowledge (*gnosis*) that will enable his ascent to the upper world of true knowledge and salvation:

> The Blessed one, the Mother-Father, the beneficent and merciful, had mercy [on Adam]. . . . So through his beneficent Spirit and his great mercy, he sent a helper to Adam. She is luminous Thought, who is from him (and) who is called Life (= Eve). It is she who aids the whole creation by toiling with him, guiding him by correction toward his fullness, and teaching him about the descent of the seed and teaching him about the path of ascent, the path which it had come down. (*Secret Revelation of John* 18.19–27)

The ideal form of Eve, as "luminous Thought," later transforms herself into the form of an eagle and sits atop the Tree of Knowledge, where she instructs the earthly Adam and Eve in the way of true knowledge:

> In the form of an eagle, I appeared on the Tree of Knowledge . . . so that I might teach them and awaken them from the depth of the sleep. For they were both in a fallen state and they recognized

their nakedness. Thought appeared to them as light, awakening their thought. (*Secret Revelation of John* 21.26–33)

In this Gnostic revision of the Garden of Eden story, God (Yaldabaoth) shows his ignorance and malice by prohibiting Adam from eating from the Tree of Knowledge. The God above sends "Thought" to instruct Adam and Eve to eat from this tree, so that they can transcend the evil of the material world and escape the bondage of its deluded creators. The Garden of Eden story is turned inside out—its hidden philosophical meaning is the opposite of its plain or material sense. The biblical God is not the true God—he is a lower God, jealous, angry, and weak. The higher God is the "holy and perfect Mother-Father" and the "perfect Mind," and the fruit of the Tree of Knowledge is the secret path to wisdom and spiritual release in the upper world. This secret path is revealed by "Thought," the ideal form of Eve. (In other Gnostic texts it is revealed by the serpent, as the earthly form of Wisdom.)

The Secret Revelation of John is an esoteric interpretation of Genesis mingled with the Platonic theology of the Gospel of John. According to the prologue of the Gospel of John, Christ is a being of the higher world, a spiritual light that assumed material form and descended to earth:

the Word was with God, and the Word was God, through whom all things came into being, and without whom nothing came into being. . . . He was the true light, which enlightens everyone. . . . and the Word became flesh. (John 1:1–14)

The Gospel of John recasts Genesis 1:1 into a revelation of the preexistent, perfect Christ. In the Gnostic revision of Genesis, the clash between the invisible world above—where God and Christ dwell—and the material world below—where we seem to dwell—takes on new dimensions. This lower world is now an evil prison, ruled by malign and ignorant gods. The goal of Gnostic wisdom is spiritual ascent to the true light of the perfect world.

The Luminous Body

Plato's philosophy was not just a system of thought but was more importantly a way of life. The *Republic* is a vast recipe for an ideal society that will produce true philosophers. Platonic philosophy is a life discipline, which enables its practitioner to perceive the true world above and to lead a good life below. Similarly, the Platonic Genesis is not just a system of knowledge but, as Philo of Alexandria shows clearly, a philosophical recipe for an enlightened life.

The body plays an important role in these life practices. For Plato, the divine craftsman created this world to be a good world, but was constrained by the limitations of physical matter. Philo and other Platonists often describe the body as a prison of the soul, as in the allegorical interpretation of God's call to Abraham:

> Go forth, then, from the earthly matter that envelops you. Escape, man, from the abominable prison, your body, and from the pleasures and lusts that act as its jailers. (*Migration of Abraham*, 9)

The Gnostic interpreters of Genesis intensify the denigration of the body to include the whole material world as a prison, created by a malicious god. The Platonic duality of the sensible and the intelligible—the flesh and the soul—becomes dizzyingly complicated in the world of Yaldabaoth and company.

The most extreme practitioners of a life discipline drawn from the mixture of Platonism and Genesis were the Christian ascetics known as the Desert Fathers. Their practices of self-denial and mortification of the flesh arose in the Egyptian desert in the fourth century CE. It is not a coincidence that the Gnostic Gospels were hidden in the Egyptian desert, outside the monastery at Nag Hammadi, by ascetic monks at this time, nor is it a coincidence that a translation of Plato's *Republic* was bound together with the Gnostic texts. The Platonic refiguring of Genesis was part of the religious environment for these seekers of salvation in the desert.

The Desert Fathers fasted, prayed, and battled against the demons of passion, anger, and lust. Some never spoke. Their bodies were emaciated and scarred with disease; their clothes were rags. They dwelled in caves or makeshift cells. And yet observers described their life as perfect and angelic, as if they were living the life of Adam in paradise. As Peter Brown explains this paradoxical situation:

> The ascetics imposed severe restraints on their bodies because they were convinced that they could sweep the body into a desperate venture. . . . [T]he men of the desert were thought capable of recovering, in the hushed silence of that dead landscape, a touch of the unimaginable glory of Adam's first state.[15]

Like the Essene ascetics of Qumran, the Desert Fathers sought to regain the glory of Adam through discipline and prayer. But their degree of physical renunciation far surpassed the Essene rules. The Qumran community separated itself from civilization to purify itself and prepare for the end of days. But there is no mortification of the flesh in the Qumran discipline, nor is there a belief that the body is a prison of the soul. The duality at Qumran is not matter versus spirit but the duality of good and evil forces *within* the body: "Until now the spirits of truth and injustice feud in the heart of man" (*Rule of the Community* [IQS] iv.23). At the grand transformation of the end-time, God will "rip out all spirit of injustice from the innermost part of his flesh, and cleanse him with the spirit of holiness" (iv.20–21). The body is not the culprit. The theory and practice of ascetic transformation are different for the Desert Fathers.

According to one of these Fathers, John Climacus, the desert ascetics were battling their own material nature:

> The monk finds himself in an earthly and defiled body, but pushes himself into the rank and status of the incorporeal angels. . . . Withdrawal from the world is a willing hatred of all that is materially prized, a denial of nature for the sake of what is above nature. (*Ladder of Divine Ascent*)[16]

If the ascetic wins the battle with his earthly nature, the prize is a transformation to the angelic, luminous body of Adam. Brown describes the motivating idea of Adam's original body:

> Adam's physical body had been unimaginably different from our own. It had been a faithful mirror of a soul which, itself, mirrored the utterly undivided, untouched simplicity of God. . . . It was like the diaphanous radiance of a still midday sky.[17]

The luminous glow of Adam's body—which was the perfect container for his unblemished soul—explains why the most perfect of the Desert Fathers are described as shining with "the likeness of the glory of Adam":

> They said of Abba Pambo, that just as Moses had taken on the likeness of the glory of Adam, when

his face shone with the glory of the Lord, in the same way, the face of Abba Pambo shone like lightning. (*Sayings of the Fathers* 12.372)[18]

Similarly, other holy Fathers (*abba* is Aramaic for "father") are described as having luminous bodies. Abba Or's "face was so radiant that the sight of him alone filled one with awe."[19] A monk looked into the window of Abba Arsenius's cell, and he saw the old man as a "flame."[20] When Abba Joseph raised his hands, "his fingers became like ten torches of fire, and he said, 'If you will, you shall be made wholly a flame.'"[21] Each of these Desert Fathers has shed his shadow-body and achieved the glorious body of Adam, which existed prior to Adam's fall into the world of suffering and death, and which will once more clothe the righteous at the end of time.

Yet it would seem to our eyes that the bodies of the Desert Fathers were wretched and tormented. How can mortified bodies be described as luminous? Here we see the duality of the Platonic body. The grotesque bodies of the Desert Fathers were only sensible, material objects, which obscured the higher reality of their intelligible bodies. As Patricia Miller writes, "asceticism can be understood as an attempt to manipulate the 'dim' body so as to drive it as close as possible toward. . . . [t]he body of plenitude."[22]

The Desert Fathers were, in a sense, "performance artists, enacting the spiritual body in the here and now."[23] Through this corporeal performance, the appearance of the physical body of the emaciated Desert Father triggered a vision of his intelligible body, which is luminous and perfect. Since the visible is the shadow of the real, the Fathers disciplined their shadow-bodies in order to unveil on earth their real spiritual bodies. The disfigured body becomes a cryptic sign—like the cryptic words of Scripture—which, to the enlightened eye, reveals its higher being.

The bodies of the Desert Fathers were Platonic bodies, consisting of the duality of the sensible and the intelligible. At the same time they were Adamic bodies, descended from the first man who once possessed a luminous body but lost it when his willfulness, gluttony, and passion overcame him. The Desert Fathers sought to regain Adam's luminous body by disciplining their wills and bodies in the harsh open desert. As paradoxical as it seems, their hard life was a paradise regained. As Palladius writes of these desert heroes, their lives are "sufficient proof of the resurrection," since they had already achieved luminous and imperishable bodies and lived in paradise.[24]

With the Desert Fathers, we see a confluence of Platonic worlds and apocalyptic expectation. The luminous bodies of these spiritual adepts provided a glimpse of the glorious end-time for all the righteous, clothed in Adam's glory. Many pilgrims went to the desert in search of the Desert Fathers, seeking a glimpse of their perfect life. Palladius writes that he "looked into every cave and hut of the monks of the desert with accurate and pious intent,"[25] hoping to gaze upon their angelic bodies. The secret bodies of the Desert Fathers were signs of the end-time *and* the higher reality of the intelligible world. In their lives of humility and spiritual grace, the apocalyptic and the Platonic senses of Genesis come together.

Between the Figure and the Real

CHAPTER 5

"Hurtaly was in truth never actually inside Noah's
  Ark—he could never have got in: he was too
  big—but he did sit astride it with a leg on either
  side like little children on their hobby-horses."

Sometime between the medieval and early modern world, the figural sense of Genesis became strained and began to break. The figural sense began to yield to a simpler, more realistic sense. But with the decline of the figural sense, new problems arose in the life of Genesis. The hidden meanings of Genesis, which were most palpable during the Middle Ages, became endangered. Not all of these controversies were focused on Genesis, but as the central text in medieval cosmology and history, its foundational stories were always in play.

The Figural World

In the *Inferno*, the greatest poem of the Middle Ages, Dante has a strange encounter with the Three Furies, deadly goddesses in Greek mythology, who threaten him in the fifth circle of Hell. He pauses for a moment to address his readers:

> O you who have sound intellects,
> consider the teaching that is hidden
> behind the veil of these strange verses.
> (Inferno 9.61–63)[1]

While shielding his eyes from the fierce goddesses, Dante pauses for a moment to point out the figural nature of his text. His strange verses, he says, are veils behind which lie hidden meanings. It requires a "sound intellect" to detect these secret meanings. The kind of reading that Dante recommends is comparable to reading Scripture—and Dante was deliberately writing a vernacular Scripture—with one important difference. His poetry consists of, as he says elsewhere, "a truth hidden beneath a beautiful lie" (*Convivio* II.1.3).[2] Scripture, in contrast, contains truth hidden beneath another truth. It is a two-layered truth, one layer expressed in the sensible words and the other in the veiled meanings behind them.

This sense of the doubled truth of Scripture had been codified by Augustine in the fifth century, most famously in his great treatise, *The City of God*, written shortly after the Goths sacked Rome. Augustine embraced the figural senses of Scripture—including the apocalyptic and Platonic senses—but also stipulated that the sensible words are testimony to historical facts. That is, both layers of the twofold sense of Scripture—the literal and the figural—are simultaneously true. There can be multiple figural meanings as long one adheres to the truth of the sensible words. In this he was objecting to the thoroughgoing allegorists, such as Philo and Origen, who denied the truth of the plain sense when it conflicted with reason.

In his comments on the Garden of Eden story, Augustine accepts both the Platonic and apocalyptic (or, as he calls them, the "symbolic" and the "prophetic") senses of the story, but maintains the necessity of the historical sense:

No one can stop us from interpreting Paradise symbolically as the life of the blessed; its four rivers as the four virtues . . . the fruit of the trees as the character of the righteous; the Tree of Life as Wisdom. . . . We can also interpret the details of Paradise with reference to the Church, which gives them a better significance as prophetic indications of things to come in the future. Thus Paradise stands for the Church itself . . . the four rivers represent the four Gospels; the fruit trees, the saints; and the fruit, their achievements; the Tree of Life, the holy of holies, must be Christ himself. . . . and there may be other more valuable lines of interpretation. There is no prohibition against such exegesis, provided that we also believe in the truth of the story as a faithful record of historical fact. (*City of God* 13.21)[3]

Augustine grants the accuracy of the hidden meanings of the text, as long as the historical meaning of the sensible words is not in doubt. The Platonic sense includes the four virtues and Wisdom, as it does for Philo. The apocalyptic sense includes Christ and the Church as the agents of future salvation. Augustine grants that there may be more interpretations still, a potentially endless number, all signified by the true events related in Scripture.

Built into this way of reading Scripture is an important implication about the meaning of nature and history. Not only do the sensible words of Scripture have hidden meanings, but so do the events and situations that they describe. Just as the words have plain *and* cryptic senses, so too do the sensible things to which the words refer. Both words and things have plain and cryptic senses. And all these layers of meaning were all intended by the Creator.

Marie-Dominique Chenu called this dualistic perspective a "symbolist mentality."[4] The world is like a book—like The Book—whose multiple meanings were all placed there by the divine Author. The twelfth-century scholar Hugh of Saint Victor used the metaphor of the world as book: "The entire sense-perceptible world is like a book written by the finger of God . . . and each particular creature is like a figure."[5] The Platonic duality of the world conformed to the dual model of Scripture. The sensible things of the world, like the sensible words of Scripture, were richly symbolic, revealing—to those of sound intellect—the hidden senses "behind the veil of these strange verses." This symbolist mentality was pervasive in medieval Christian theology. It was also widespread in medieval Judaism, particularly in the symbolist mentality of Kabbalah.[6]

Dante's call to his intelligent readers to pierce the veil of his "strange verses" applies in the Middle Ages to the world itself—everything in God's creation is a symbol of spiritual things. As Chenu explains, "Everything was a *sacramentum* in the technical sense of the word, that is, a sign of an inner reality."[7] And so animals, stones, and plants had hidden meanings, as elaborately detailed in the medieval bestiaries and lapidaries.[8] For instance, to bring us back to Genesis, the apple signified evil, because its name in Latin (*malum*) is a homonym for "evil" (*malum*). This is why the forbidden fruit in medieval and Renaissance paintings of the Garden of Eden is always an apple—it was the fruit of *bonum et malum* ("good and evil").

The symbolism of things operates consistently in Scripture. According to Odo of Morimond, "the Divine Scripture speaks to us through the similitudes of things so that it may move us to faith."[9] Everything in Scripture—and in the world—is symbolic and potentially salvific. As Jacques Le Goff comments, "It was always a question of finding the keys which would force open the hidden world, the true and external world, the one in which men could be saved."[10]

The Excess of Symbols

The Church Father Jerome described Scripture as "an infinite forest of meanings."[11] Making one's way in this forest was a serious business, since salvation depended on it. But the proliferation of symbols caused its own problems. Who had the authority to determine which interpretations were acceptable—or were they all equally true? How could anyone find his way among the welter of interpretations? In the Middle Ages scholars compiled anthologies of interpretations by the Church Fathers, but this only made the problem of the excess of symbols more obvious.

Alan of Lille, a scholar who was keenly attuned to the vast symbolism of the world, argued that all scriptural interpretation must be supported by reason. Church authority alone was not sufficient to make an interpretation valid, since its authority could be misused. He wrote, "because authority has a wax nose, which can be bent in different ways, she must be fortified by reasons."[12] Alan was an important figure in what historians call the Renaissance of the twelfth century, a period when learning flourished and the first universities were founded. It was a time of renewed study of languages, logic, and the humanities. Theological inquiry became allied with the new learning—consider Alan's marvelous geometrical aphorism: "God is the intelligible sphere, whose center is everywhere and circumference nowhere."[13] Theology and biblical interpretation were "fortified by reasons" as the new learning gained authority.

During the twelfth century the interpretation of Genesis in both Christian and Jewish circles underwent a radical shift. A decisive figure was the French Jewish rabbi Solomon ben Isaac, better known as Rashi. As Avraham Grossman explains, Rashi was deeply affected by the new learning:

There was a new confidence in the power of reason. . . . French Jewish scholars, influenced by the cultural renaissance of twelfth-century Europe and

in need of new ways to respond to Christian interpretations of the Bible, were willing to embrace
new methods.[14]

Rashi's new method gave prominence to what he
called the "plain sense" (*peshaṭ*) of Scripture. He possessed acute linguistic knowledge, based on the Hebrew scholarship of Spanish Jews, who had adopted
the methods of Arabic scholarship in Spain. Rashi's
focus on the grammatical and contextual analysis of
Hebrew words and his Renaissance respect for analytical reason created an awareness of the gap between the
figural interpretations of rabbinic authorities and the
"plain sense" of the text. In his biblical commentary,
Rashi cites rabbinic interpretations only when they
suit the plain sense, and where none were suitable, he
provides his own.

Rashi states his goal as follows:

> There are many Midrashic interpretations , and our
> Rabbis have already collected them in their appro-
> priate order in *Genesis Rabbah* and in other Mi-
> drashic books. As for me, I am only concerned
> with the plain sense of Scripture and the Midrashic
> interpretations that explain the words of Scripture
> in a fitting manner. (*Commentary on Genesis* 3:8)[15]

Rashi's explains the concept of the "plain sense" as
"interpretations that explain the words of Scripture in
a fitting manner." The last phrase, which I have trans-

lated (following Grossman) as "in a fitting manner," literally means "a word spoken according to its circumstance" (*davar davur 'al 'ofnaw*). As Rashi explains elsewhere, he is referring to the semantic context and the rules of grammar. In other words, the criteria for Scriptural interpretation are reasons that derive from the use of language. Rashi seeks to explain the plain sense of the text according to it grammar, context, and the meaning of words. There are no other criteria—if it doesn't "fit" these criteria, then an interpretation doesn't apply. As he says in his comment on Genesis 10:25, "Scripture is not concerned to hide, but to clearly explain (*lefaresh*)." That is to say, there are no hidden or cryptic meanings. This is a revolutionary claim.

In his Genesis commentary, Rashi often criticizes interpretations that swerve from the plain meaning. Dozens of times he writes: "There are Midrashic interpretations, but they do not suit the plain sense" (at Genesis 3:22, etc.); or more simply, "There are many Midrashic interpretations" (at Genesis 5:1, etc.). Rashi does not cite these interpretations, but he grants that they exist. This is one way to cope with the excess of figural interpretations—by omitting the ones that fail to fit the sensible text.

But sometimes Rashi does include one or two figural interpretations of a verse, which he contrasts with his explanation of the plain sense. Curiously, sometimes he cites a rabbinic interpretation that clearly diverges from the plain sense, without providing his own explanation. Rashi seems to be fond of these figural interpretations, even though they swerve from the plain sense of the text.

Consider the following examples from Genesis. In the Garden of Eden story, when God decides to create for Adam a "helper corresponding to him" (*ezer kenegdo*), Rashi cites a Midrashic interpretation (from *Genesis Rabbah* 17.3) that breaks up the two-word phrase and concocts a homily:

> If he is virtuous, (she is) a helper (*ezer*). If he is not, (she is) against him (*kenegdo*), to fight him. (*Commentary on Genesis* 2:18)

This interpretation is not what the words "helper corresponding to him" really mean. In his selection from rabbinic interpretation, Rashi often includes interpretations that he likes, irrespective of whether they "explain the words of Scripture in a fitting manner."

On the first day of Creation, at the point when "God saw that the light was good, and God separated the light from the darkness," Rashi comments:

> With this we must rely on the words of [Midrashic] interpretation. He saw that it was not fitting that the wicked should use it [the light], and He separated it for the righteous in the Future to Come [*Genesis Rabbah* 3.6]. But according to its plain sense, explain it as follows: He saw that it was good, and therefore it was unfitting that it [the light] and darkness should function in mingled

confusion, so he established that this one is bounded by day and the other by night. (*Commentary on Genesis* 1:4)

Here Rashi hedges the contrast between the two kinds of interpretation. He provides a suitable interpretation of the plain sense, but also appeals to a figural interpretation. The Midrash about the primal light that God reserves for the righteous in the Future to Come is an apocalyptic interpretation with Platonic overtones—the Future World is one where the righteous live in a realm of transcendent light. This interpretation takes its cue from the problem that light is created on the first day of Creation but the sun is not created until the fourth day. The Midrash infers that the light of the first day must be different than the sunlight of the fourth day, and that therefore God must have hidden away this primal light until the end of time.

Rashi approves of this apocalyptic-Platonic interpretation, even though he clearly comprehends and precisely explains the plain meaning of the text. Why does he violate his own criteria in this instance? Rashi explains the plain sense, but he is not willing to dispense with the figural sense altogether. His practice is inconsistent with his stated aims, presumably because of his respect for the classical rabbis and his fondness for some of their figural interpretations.

Rashi copes with the excess of symbols by establishing principles of selection, but also by loosening his own principles when he pleases. His position oscillates between figural and realistic interpretation—sometimes criticizing the former, sometimes embracing it. He expresses "open rebuke and hidden love" for his predecessors, the classical rabbis. This is the quality that makes Rashi's commentary so beloved in Jewish tradition, since it is a compendium of interpretations that explain the words of Genesis *and* a treasury of classical Midrashic interpretation. As a result, Rashi's commentary appeals to the intellect and the imagination. There is something for everyone in it.

By invoking the claims of reason and linguistic knowledge, Rashi institutes a new method of reading Genesis for the plain senses of the text. This principle, in theory, divests the Bible of its hidden, cryptic senses, and excludes the vast forest of figural interpretations. His strategy of contextual "fit" is one way to manage the excess of symbols. But in practice Rashi is less stringent. He travels a middle path between the figural and the real, embracing the claims of reason while preserving—in reduced portions—the legacy of traditional commentary. In so doing, he pays homage to rabbinic authority while decisively revising its foundations.

The Clear Words of Scripture

Rashi's shift in focus from figural interpretation to the realism of the plain sense was carried on by his disciples—including his grandson, who became a famous scholar—and was quickly taken up by French Christians. When the French scholar Nicholas of Lyra wrote his influential *Literal Commentary on the Whole Bible* (1331), he regularly referred to the interpretations of "Rabbi Solomon."

A young Augustinian monk of the sixteenth century, Martin Luther, initially resisted Nicholas's focus on the plain sense. He later reminisced, "When I was a monk I was a master in the use of allegories. I allegorized everything . . . even a chamber pot."[16] But as his views changed—as he turned into the champion of the Protestant Reformation—he abandoned allegory: "The literal sense does it—in it there's life, comfort, power, instruction and skill. The other is foolishness, however brilliant the impression it makes."[17]

Luther's rejection of allegory and his embrace of the plain sense of the text were linked to his rejection of the authority of the Catholic Church. He embraced "Scripture alone" (*sola scriptura*) as the basis for faith and Christian life. In his reply to the accusation of heresy at the Council of Worms (1521), he sets his allegiance to Scripture in bold contrast to the fallible decrees of the Church:

> Since your Imperial Majesty and Lordships demand a simple answer I will do so without horns or teeth as follows: Unless I am convinced by the testimony of Scripture or by clear reason—for I do not trust either in the pope or in councils alone, since it is well known that they have often erred and contradicted themselves—I am bound by the

Scriptures I have quoted, and my conscience is captive to the Word of God. I cannot and will not recant.[18]

By relying solely on "the testimony of Scripture" and "clear reason," Luther rejected the authority of the Catholic Church, "since it is well known that they have often erred." Scripture and clear reason are embraced as the sole guarantors of truth. The Protestant Reformation was based on this alliance between the light of reason—here Luther shows his Renaissance heritage—and the plain sense of Scripture. Luther's rejection of tradition is a quintessentially modern gesture, but as we will see, it creates many new dilemmas, since reason sometimes conflicts with the plain sense of Scripture.

In his Genesis commentary Luther often ridicules allegorical interpretation. For instance, the Platonic interpretation of Adam and Eve as "higher reason" and "lower reason" is mocked as "a most absurd allegory." Such interpretations "utterly smother the true meaning and replace it with an idea which is not merely useless but disastrous. . . . Therefore we shall disregard such destructive and foolish absurdities."[19]

Luther has another motive for condemning allegory—it serves as an all-purpose vehicle for asserting the false claims of the Church. Pope Innocent III had declared that the "two great lights" in Genesis 1:16 are allegorical symbols of pontifical and royal authority. Luther points out—with relish—that this is a crude justification of power:

The pope deserves praise for piety and learning in the matter of allegories when he thunders thus from his exalted position: "God made two large luminaries, the sun and the moon. The sun is the papal office, from which the imperial majesty derives its light, just as the moon does from the sun." Oh, such audacious insolence and such villainous desire for power! (*Lectures on Genesis* 2.152)

Luther also criticizes the Church Fathers for indulging in allegory. For instance, when Augustine interprets the seven "days" in Genesis 1 as an allegory for the seven stages of "spiritual illumination,"

The result is no real contribution. What need is there of setting up a twofold knowledge? Nor does it serve any useful purpose to make Moses at the outset so mystical and allegorical. His purpose is to teach us, not about allegorical creatures and an allegorical world but about real creatures and a visible world apprehended by the senses. Therefore, as the proverb has it, he "calls a spade a spade," that is, he employs the terms "day" and "evening" without allegory, just as we customarily do. . . . If, then, we do not understand the nature of the days or have no insight into why God wanted to make use of these intervals of time, let us confess our lack of understanding rather than distort the words, contrary to their context, into a foreign meaning. (*Lectures on Genesis* 1.5)

Luther makes several important points here. He questions the Platonic duality at the heart of allegorical interpretation—"What need is there of setting up a two-fold knowledge?" For Luther, the plain sense of Scripture and the plain sense of the world are undeniable. The world is filled with real things, not material symbols of invisible ideas. He sees no reason to posit an ideal world hovering above the sensible world. The new learning and the realism of the Renaissance are evident in Luther's critique. The Word and the World are both real things, with no invisible double.

Once the Platonic duality of reality has gone away, the Platonic duality of Scripture has no external support, and allegorical interpretation seems like a house of cards. Luther takes great delight in blowing away the cards, which to him is an effective means of undermining the authority of the Catholic Church.

His insistence that Genesis is about "real creatures and a visible world" and is not a Platonic allegory also reflects his historical judgment about the capacities of the original audience—the people of ancient Israel. Here we detect the new historical perspective of Renaissance, which was conscious of the "pastness" of biblical Israel. He explains, "Moses wrote so that uneducated men might have clear accounts of the creation" (*Lectures on Genesis* 1.19). This is an effective criticism of figural interpretation. If Genesis was written for ancient shepherds and farmers—not for philosophers or theologians—then we must assume that it was (and is) accessible to ordinary people.

Figural interpretation is a counsel of despair, a ploy for the interpreter who does not understand the plain sense of Scripture. Luther counsels, "let us confess our lack of understanding rather than distort the words, contrary to their context, into a foreign meaning." Like Rashi, Luther appeals to the meanings of words in their context as the surest guide to the Bible's native meanings. Why distort the words when their meaning is obscure? Rather, "let us confess our lack of understanding." This is a very modern attitude toward the problems in the text.

Since for the most part the words of Scripture are tolerably clear, "I prefer what is simplest and can be understood by those with little education" (*Lectures on Genesis* 1.10). So Luther maintains that the Garden of Eden was a real place, and the four rivers of paradise were real rivers, not allegorical symbols:

> These, then, are all historical facts. This is something to which I carefully call attention, lest the unwary reader be led astray by the authority of the fathers, who give up the idea that this is history and look for allegories. (*Lectures on Genesis* 1.93)

But there is a problem with Luther's emphasis that the "clear accounts of creation" consist of "historical facts." He admits that many of the details of the Garden of Eden story seem dubious and perhaps even fictional, which is one of the reasons that the Church Fathers sought out a hidden sense. But with the figural sense excluded, Luther must wrestle with his historical judgment and submit to the authority of the plain sense of Scripture, even when it conflicts with reason and the plain sense of things: "The more it seems to conflict with all experience and reason, the more carefully it must be noted and the more surely believed" (*Lectures on Genesis* 1.125).

When faced with the creation of Eve from Adam's rib, he wonders:

> What, I ask you, could sound more like a fairy tale if you were to follow your reason? Would anyone believe this account about the creation of Eve if it were not so clearly told? . . . This is extravagant fiction and the silliest kind of nonsense if you set aside the authority of Scripture and follow the judgment of reason. (*Lectures on Genesis* 1.123)

He concludes, "Although it sounds like a fairy tale to reason, it is the most certain truth. It is revealed in the Word of God, which alone, as I said, imparts true information" (*Lectures on Genesis* 1.131).

This paradox poses a problem for Luther and later interpreters. If the twin criteria for true interpretation are "the testimony of Scripture" and "clear reason," as he said to the Council of Worms, what to do when the two conflict? Luther invokes the authority of Scripture to settle the potential conflict, but this opens further difficulties. To whom does one appeal when Scripture is obscure? Luther's answer is that the final arbiter of Scripture is its author, the Holy Spirit: "the Bible is the Holy Spirit's own peculiar book, writing and word."[20]

Its interpretation requires spiritual aid: "Scripture is to be understood only by that Spirit through which Scripture was written."[21] Thus the words and meanings of Scripture are clear, but some are clear only to its author, not to us. The authority of the Holy Spirit overrules the objections of reason and experience. And inspiration by the Holy Spirit belongs not to the Church but to the individual believer.

Luther undermined the Scriptural authority of the Church and invited all people to read and understand with faith alone the Bible's "certain, accessible, and clear" words. By providing a German translation of the Bible—which circulated widely because of the recently invented printing press—he made Scripture available to ordinary people. But by appealing to the individual's ability to interpret Scripture by the inspiration by the Holy Spirit, Luther created new problems that nearly destroyed his Reformation and that persist to this day. Too much inspiration can be dangerous.

Shortly after Luther's writings began to circulate, other reformers—called the radical Reformers—took up the task of proclaiming their interpretation of Scripture's apocalyptic secrets. They called for a revolution to restore the perfect life of Adam and Eve in paradise, prior to the invention of personal property, princes, and priests. One of their slogans was "When Adam dug and Eve spun, who was then the nobleman?" In 1524—two years after Luther was declared a heretic by the Catholic Church—a peasants' rebellion broke out in Germany. The peasants were not only throwing off the yoke of papal and royal authority, they were also jump-starting the apocalyptic battle of the end-time. The initial victories of the untrained peasant armies were short-lived. Nearly a hundred thousand peasants were massacred by royal troops.

For Luther, these rebellions were "the devil's work." In his infamous pamphlet *Against the Robbing and Murdering Hordes of Peasants*, he condemned the radical prophets and their followers. He railed against their biblical interpretation. The idyllic picture of Creation in Genesis, he declared, does not support the rejection of wealth, property, and princes: "It does not help the peasants when they pretend that according to Genesis 1 and 2 all things were created free and common."[22] The Garden of Eden should not be taken as a revolutionary manifesto. And he warned the rebels of retribution, since "the destruction of the world is to be expected every hour."[23] As Luther learned to his dismay, the ideals of "Scripture alone," "faith alone," the priesthood of all believers," and "the gift of the Holy Spirit" combine to make a volatile mixture. As Luther replied to his revolutionary archrival Thomas Müntzer:

> Bibel, Babel, Bubel. You say it won't do any good to have gobbled a thousand Bibles. I tell you that unless you can cite clear words of Scripture for your doings, I will not listen to you, even though you have swallowed the Holy Ghost, feathers and all.[24]

But the "clear words of Scripture" were no match for the fire of apocalyptic zeal.[25]

The peasant rebellions were brutally suppressed. Meanwhile the Protestant movement was splintering into innumerable denominations. Soon Europe was divided between Protestant and Catholic territories, and a century of religious wars commenced. The conflicting interpretations of Scripture had become a path to irrationality, bloodshed, and war.

The Comedy of the Real

One honest response to the lunacy of the world is to laugh. Laughter relieves anxiety and fear, and it pokes holes in the pretensions of the powerful. In medieval times, humor was often coarse and obscene, and was effective because of it. Luther's rough handling of his opponents is rooted in this medieval tradition. During the heyday of the Reformation, with social upheaval, religious conflict, and the devil on the loose, François Rabelais wrote the first volume of his comic novel *Gargantua and Pantagruel*. As Mikhail Bakhtin observes, "Medieval laughter found its highest expression in Rabelais' novel."[26] It was an immediate best-seller.

"Rabelaisian laughter," M. A. Screech writes, "is both a complement to Luther's scornful vehemence and an antidote to it."[27] Rabelais was a doctor and former Benedictine monk who satirized the conventional wisdom of his time. He took great delight in parodying the Bible and contemporary religious disputes. John Calvin and the Catholic censors agreed on one thing: Rabelais was a heretic. (But he wasn't—he was a learned Catholic who was mercilessly funny.) Calvin decried Rabelais as "a rustic who makes vile jokes at the expense of Holy Writ."[28] And the first edition of the Catholic *Index of Prohibited Books* in 1564 placed Rabelais at the head of "heretics of the first class."

The book of Genesis plays an important comic role in the first volume, *The Horrifying and Dreadful Deeds and Prowess of the Most Famous Pantagruel, King of the Dipsodes, Son of the Great Giant Gargantua* (1532). The hero, Pantagruel, is descended from the biblical giants, who were the offspring of the Sons of God and the daughters of men in Genesis 6:1–4 (these children are called *gigantes*, "giants," in the Septuagint). The narrator begins the book in good biblical fashion with Pantagruel's genealogy, but first with a nod to the great benefactor of humankind, Noah:

> Noah—that sainted man to whom we are all beholden and indebted since it was he who planted the vine from which comes to us that nectar-like, precious, heavenly, joyful and deifying liquor that we call wine.[29]

To Rabelais (and doubtless many others), Noah was a saint because of his "nectar-like" invention, wine. The Reformers, in contrast, deplored drunkenness. Luther wrote, "If anyone wishes to imitate Noah and get drunk, he deserves to go to hell."[30] Rabelais turns upside-down this dour sensibility (although Luther, in real life, appreciated good beer and wine).

In good biblical fashion, the narrator relates Pantagruel's genealogy, which includes many illustrious giant ancestors:

> The first of whom was Charlbroth,
> Who begat Sarabroth,
> Who begat Faribroth,
> Who begat Hurtaly, who was a good eater of sops
>   and ruled from the time of the Flood . . .
> Who begat Eryx, who invented the game of
>   thimblerig . . .
> Who begat Etion who . . . was the first to catch the
>   pox through not having drunk his wine cool in
>   summer . . .
> Who begat Gabbara, who first invented matching
>   drink for drink . . .
> Who begat Offot, who developed an awesomely
>   fine nose from drinking straight from the
>   wine-cask . . .
> Who begat Gemmagog, who invented long-toed
>   Crakow shoes . . .
> Who begat Morgan, who was the first in the world
>   ever to play dice wearing glasses . . .
> Who begat Gob-fly, who was the first to invent the
>   smoking of ox-tongues in the chimney: before
>   him they were salted like hams . . .
> Who begat Gayoffe, whose bollocks were of poplar
>   and whose cock was of mountain-ash . . .

Who begat Galahad, who was the inventor of
    flagons . . .
Who begat Garnet-cock,
Who begat Grand-gullet,
Who begat Gargantua,
Who begat the noble Pantagruel, my master.[31]

This extravagant and hilarious genealogy is a parody of
the (usually tedious) biblical genealogies, which include a few ancient inventors:

Ada gave birth to Jabal, who was the father of
those who dwell in tents and have livestock. His
brother's name was Jubal, who was the father of all
those who play the lyre and pipe. Zillah bore
Tubal-Cain, who was the father of those who made
all kinds of metal tools. (Genesis 4:20–22)

Genesis neglects to tell us who invented thimblerig,
long-toed shoes, flagons, drinking games, and the
smoking of ox-tongues, so Rabelais's narrator helpfully
fills in these gaps in his comic expansion of Genesis.

The narrator then turns to a difficult interpretive
problem—how did the giant Hurtaly survive the
Flood, since he is not listed in Genesis as having been
in the ark? As a good Renaissance exegete, the narrator
finds a solution from Jewish tradition:

I was not there at the time to tell you about it as I
would like to, so I will cite the authority of the
Massoretes, those fine, well-hung and beautiful

Hebrew windbags who affirm that Hurtaly was in truth never actually inside Noah's Ark—he could never have got in: he was too big—but that he did sit astride it with a leg on either side like little children on their hobby-horses. . . . In that way Hurtaly saved the aforesaid Ark from foundering, for he propelled it with his legs, turning it with his foot whichever way he would as one does with the rudder of a boat.[32]

This interpretation is adapted from a Jewish legend about the giant Og's journey on the Ark.[33] The narrator then mocks his own erudite but far-fetched interpretation:

> Did you understand all that? Then down a good swig without water! For if you believe it or not, *"Neither do I," said she.*[34]

The unidentified woman ("she") who interrupts the narrator seems not to believe it, and neither does the narrator, who recommends a swig of drink. Having parodied the Flood story and its contemporary interpretation, the narrator returns to the genealogy of his mock-biblical hero: "Gargantua, at the age of four hundred and four score four and forty, begat Pantagruel."

Genesis is the object of parody here, as is the contemporary manner of handling interpretive problems in the Flood story. Rabelais knew his Bible well, as did his Renaissance audience. A good comic pokes fun at the familiar and the sacrosanct, and the stories of Genesis were both. Although Calvin fumed against Rabelais as a "condemner of God," Rabelais was really criticizing the pretentious piety of his time. His laughter unmasked foolish prattling about the Bible and everything else. His comic iconoclastic style and his fondness for sensual pleasure struck a responsive chord in his readers and patrons, among whom were Catholic bishops and royalty.

Although his heroes and their adventures are fantastic and larger than life, Rabelais's book is one of the first modern works of fiction whose hallmark is realism. Pantagruel and his bawdy friends are not symbols of something else, but revel in earthy reality. There are no Platonic worlds here. The world is strictly material, and populated by sensible—and sexual—bodies.

Rablelais openly ridicules allegory in the preface to his second book, *Gargantua* (whose motto is "Live joyfully!"). In mock-theological style, he advises the reader to read his book for its hidden senses,

> for you will discover therein a very different savor and a more hidden instruction which will reveal to you the highest hidden truths and the most awesome mysteries touching upon our religion as well as upon matters of state and family life.[35]

Having revealed to the reader that there are "hidden truths and the most awesome mysteries" in his book, the narrator then proceeds to mock the very idea of finding such allegories in other books:

> Now do you really and truly believe that Homer, when composing the *Iliad* and the *Odyssey*, had any thought of the allegories which have been caulked on to him by Plutarch, Heraclides of Pontus, Eustathius or Conutus and which Politian purloined from them? If you do so believe, then you come by neither foot nor hand close to my own opinion.[36]

The book cited for the absurdity of allegory is Homer—not Genesis—but the message is the same: Those who read books for the hidden allegorical sense are fools. The figural reading of "these merry new Chronicles" is equally absurd:

> I was no more thinking of such things when I wrote them than you were, who were perhaps having a drink just as I was! . . . Expound therefore all my words and deeds in the most perfect of senses; hold in reverence the cheese-shaped brain which feeds you this for tripe and, insofar as in you lies, keep me ever merry.[37]

The narrator has come full circle. After proclaiming the existence of hidden meanings in his book, he now admits that he wrote the book while drinking, which is "the appropriate time for writing of these high topics and profound teachings." The narrator is teasing us with the promise of hidden meanings, while ridiculing such reading practices as absurd and extolling the bodily focus of his book. No allegorical meanings about invisible worlds, only the "deeds and prowess" of his ribald heroes in a very sensible world.

Erich Auerbach aptly describes the embrace of the real in Rabelais's novel, which breaks from the figural tradition of earlier literature. Rabelais's comic style

> permitted him to touch upon things that shocked the reactionary authorities of his time, to display them in a twilight between jest and earnest. . . . And above all, it precisely served his purpose— namely, a fruitful irony which confuses the customary aspects and proportions of things, which makes the real appear in the super-real, wisdom in folly, rebellion in a cheerful and flavorful acceptance of life; which, through the play of possibilities, casts a dawning light on the possibility of freedom.[38]

By his exuberant super-realism, his mockery of allegory, and his comical parody of everything sacred—including and especially Genesis—Rabelais invents a modern attitude. With his earthy laughter, he mocks the very idea of the figural interpretation of the Word and the World. Things are really as they seem, with all their reserves of pleasure and pain. Rabelais seals the demise of the figural sense with his laughter. The world is where we are—there is no hidden invisible world behind it. We can choose to despair or laugh at this finite world. Pantagruelists choose laughter.

Questioning the Assumptions

The life of Genesis changed utterly in the transition from the figuralism of the Middle Ages to the realism that emerged, in fits and starts, during the Renaissances of the twelfth and sixteenth centuries. Rashi, Luther, and Rabelais are major figures. But this is not a story of "great men," but of changes—both gradual and sudden—in the mental landscape. There are many direct and indirect causes for these changes, including economic forces and technology, such as the rise of guilds, urban life, and widespread trade in the eleventh and twelfth centuries and similar changes, including the invention of the printing press, in the fifteenth and sixteenth centuries. The world became larger and more complex from contact with other cultures: the earlier Renaissance was influenced by the Golden Age of Islam, and the later Renaissance encountered the New World. Changes in the mental landscape were inevitable.

We can gauge the extent of these changes in the life of Genesis by considering the new fragility of the four assumptions that had guided interpreters for over a millennium, since the melding of Jewish and Greek cultures. The rising trajectory of the figural sense in

Late Antiquity and the Middle Ages now turned into a steep decline. Rashi and Luther criticized figural interpretation, and Rabelais mocked it. Let us survey the now shaky grounds beneath the four assumptions—that the Bible is cryptic, relevant, perfect, and divine—in the wake of the two Renaissances.

Cryptic

According to Rashi, "Scripture is not concerned to hide, but to clearly explain" (*Commentary on Genesis* 10:25). His biblical commentary proceeds on this assumption, which pointedly contradicts traditional practice. But he accompanies his commentary with a rich selection of traditional Midrashic interpretations. Rashi may have regarded these imaginative interpretations as rabbinic homilies that supplement the plain meanings of the text. (Luther too, when in a charitable mood, regarded allegorical interpretations as homiletical "decoration.") Rashi clearly valued the classical rabbis—his compendious commentary on the Talmud makes this clear. But his insistence on the plain sense undermined the principle that Scripture is intrinsically cryptic.

As part of the theological and political program of his Reformation, Luther embraced the "clear words of Scripture," and rejected allegorical interpretation. He accused Church authorities of using such interpretation for their own devilish purposes. Luther sometimes indulges in mild allegory, which he regarded as harmless if not taken seriously. For instance, he halfheartedly argues that the two birds that Noah sends out from the Ark—the raven and the dove—are symbols of his favorite duality, law versus grace (*Lectures on Genesis* 2.158–64). He also held that hints of apocalyptic prophecy—authored by the Holy Spirit—were a part of the historical sense of Scripture. (Since apocalyptic interpretation is part of the New Testament, he could not dispense with it altogether.) But generally he regarded the search for cryptic meanings as "empty speculations and froth" (*Lectures on Genesis* 1.233).

During the Renaissance and Reformation, the idea that Scripture was an essentially cryptic text that required a search for hidden meanings became problematic. Many interpreters continued to derive cryptic meanings from Scripture—particularly in mystical, apocalyptic, and pietistic movements—but it was no longer a self-evident assumption. In the official circles of the Catholic Church, commitment to the cryptic senses lasted for another generation, but the force of the Reformation critique had its effect. By the time of the Galileo affair, as we will see in the next chapter, appeal to the allegorical sense was no longer viable. In Judaism, the commentaries of Renaissance scholars such as Obadiah Sforno renewed Rashi's commitment to scriptural realism in Jewish scholarship. The cryptic sense persisted only in movements that resisted the lure of modernity, as remains the case today.

Relevant

Without recourse to cryptic senses, many texts in Genesis are not obviously relevant for the present. Consider, for instance, the genealogies. After some cursory comments on the genealogy of the Edomites in Genesis 36, Rashi writes: "[Scripture] has described for you the settlements of Esau and his descendants in a brief manner, because they were not notable or important enough to explain clearly how they settled" (*Commentary on Genesis* 37:1). This chunk of genealogy is "not notable or important," which explains why Scripture describes it in a hurry. Rashi's explanation is lucid, but the result is that we need not pay attention to this text, because it has no particular value for the present.

Luther regards the genealogies as relevant only within the large-scale structure of Scripture. About the genealogies in Genesis 10, he writes, "the tenth chapter is seemingly barren and appears to serve no purpose." But he manages to find intimations of human sin and Christ in this list, and concludes, "This very chapter, even though it is considered full of dead words, has in it the thread that is drawn from the first world to the middle and the end of all things."[39] He finds a thread of significance in the linkage between beginning and end—from Adam to Christ—but this middle section itself seems "full of dead words." It is, of course, these barren words that Rabelais parodies in the ribald genealogy of Pantagruel.

Luther's contrast between "law" and "gospel" in biblical texts makes it clear that many texts—those that simply relate "law"—are irrelevant for Christians. Hence his famous remark that the Epistle of James is an "epistle of straw," and his dismissal of the book of Esther: "There is too much Judaism in [it] and not a little heathenism."[40] There are irrelevant parts of the Bible, which the discerning reader can safely ignore. The old assumption that everything is relevant has been cast aside.

Perfect

Due to the diligence of Renaissance scholarship, Luther was aware of mistakes and inconsistencies in the Bible. He responded that the main doctrines are clear, even if there are errors in the details: "The Holy Ghost has an eye only to the substance and is not bound by words."[41] Luther is not disturbed by minor imperfections or contradictions among stories: "such points do not bother me particularly."[42] Where the biblical characters misbehave, as in the story of Noah's drunkenness, he comments, "This I simply cannot excuse."[43] There is no sugar-coating of the imperfections in the text or in its heroes.

For Luther and other Renaissance readers, the words and events of Scripture may be imperfect, but these are relatively minor matters that are not necessary for salvation. The faithful reader simply has to focus on the substance, not the objectionable or imperfect details. With the ready availability of Scripture in vernacular translations, and with the decline in the Church's interpretive authority, the old assumption that Scripture is perfect in every part no longer holds.

The weave of Scripture now has noticeable knots and holes, which cannot be patched by an application of hidden meanings.

Divine

Rashi and Luther did not question the divine origins of Genesis. This question may have been unthinkable for Jews and Christians in their time. The words of Genesis came from God, who dictated them to Moses, his prophet. Both Rashi and Luther knew that there was a problem with the last chapter of the Pentateuch, which relates the death of Moses. Following older tradition, both inferred that this portion was written by Joshua. The fourth assumption, the divinity of Scripture, was the last one standing.

A century later this assumption came under scrutiny by a heretical Jewish philosopher, Baruch Spinoza. In his notorious *Theological-Political Treatise*—which was immediately banned and became an underground best-seller—Spinoza follows Rashi and Luther in criticizing those who find hidden meanings in Scripture. Interpreters of the cryptic senses of Scripture inevitably reproduce Platonic or Aristotelian ideas, which Spinoza regards as nonsense. Spinoza mockingly dissects these motives:

> Since they did not wish to appear to be following pagans, they adapted the Scriptures to them. It was insufficient for them to be mouthing nonsense themselves, they also desired . . . to render the prophets equally nonsensical.[44]

So much for the allegorical blending of Scripture and Greek philosophy. Then Spinoza takes the fateful next step:

> Most of them take it as a fundamental principle . . . that Scripture is true and divine throughout. But of course this is the very thing that should emerge from a critical examination and understanding of Scripture. It would be much better to derive it from Scripture itself, which has no need of human fabrications, but they assume it at the very beginning as a rule of interpretation.[45]

Here Spinoza appeals to the authorities of Scripture and reason, as Luther had done in his defense at Worms, and transforms their bond into a program for the "critical examination and understanding of Scripture." Luther's claim that the meaning of Scripture should be derived from Scripture itself, not from religious authorities, now changes into a call to examine Scripture by the clear light of reason. The question now posed—is it rationally warranted to believe that the Bible is true and divine?—can be addressed by reason alone.

Rashi, Luther, and Rabelais had criticized the first three assumptions; the last assumption—the Bible as a divine book—now came under question. The mental climate of the seventeenth and eighteenth centuries—when Spinoza's treatise on the Bible became a sensation—was no longer conducive to easy acceptance of any of the four assumptions. For those who continued to hold them true, there was disturbing awareness that other people were questioning them. The four assumptions became—and remain—a matter of contentious dispute. During the Renaissances they gradually became visible, rather than an invisible backdrop. They were no longer just implicit in everyday life, like the air we breathe. Once all four assumptions come under question, the life of Genesis becomes part of a new debate about the nature of God, nature, reason, and reality.

Genesis and Science: From the Beginning to Fundamentalism

"God made the two great lights—the greater light to rule the day and the lesser light to rule the night—and the stars. And God set them in the vault of heaven."

Modern science was born in the sixteenth and seventeenth centuries with the astonishing discoveries by Copernicus, Galileo, Newton, and their colleagues. Its first milestone was Copernicus's treatise *On the Revolutions of the Celestial Spheres* (1543), which presents his theory that the earth and the other planets revolve around the sun. When news of these ideas began to spread, Martin Luther had a reaction that was typical for his time and his temperament. He was annoyed:

> There is talk of a new astrologer who wants to prove that the earth moves and goes around, not heaven or the firmament, sun, and moon. . . . The fool wants to turn the whole art of astronomy upside down. However, as Holy Scripture tells us, Joshua bid the sun to stand still and not the earth.[1]

Luther was a learned man, but, as he well knew, a heliocentric universe conflicts with the plain meaning of the Bible. A new conflict was brewing. The conflict was not just about the Bible and the heliocentric model. It was over how to understand God, nature, religious and political authority, and reality. To understand the stakes of this quarrel—which has shaped the life of Genesis for nearly half a millennium—we need to take both Genesis and modern science seriously. So we turn back to the Beginning.

The Great Lights

Genesis 1 describes a picture of the universe that fits well with our ordinary senses, unaided by telescopes, satellites, and other modern contrivances. As we have seen (chapter 1), it is a well-structured and harmonious description, which draws upon and refines earlier concepts of the cosmos. The most striking innovation of this Creation account is the absolute distinction between God and the cosmos. God stands apart from nature and organizes it from the raw materials of primeval chaos. God is the agent of Creation, and nature is his object. The multifarious material world is a product of intelligent design. To the extent that this is an analytical and descriptive model of the cosmos, we may call Genesis 1 a work of ancient science. As we will see, however, it is not compatible with modern science. The discoveries of modern astronomy, geology, and biology are not dreamed of in Genesis.

Let us look at how ancient concepts of the cosmos were refined in Genesis 1. The description of the sky and the heavenly bodies—what we may call the "celestial science" of Genesis 1—derives from the general ideas of ancient Near Eastern astronomy in the first millennium BCE. The sky is a solid rotating object, shaped like a plate or inverted bowl, into which the gods have set the sun, moon, planets, and stars. An Assyrian text from the seventh century BCE describes the surface of the "lower heaven" as a solid body of sky-blue jasper stone, on which the god Marduk has inscribed the constellations: "The lower heaven is jasper. It belongs to the stars. He drew the constellations of the gods on it."[2] According to ancient astronomy, the heavenly bodies were divine things, created by the gods and usually regarded as gods themselves. Notice that we still refer to the planets by their god-names: Mercury, Venus, Mars, Jupiter, Saturn, Uranus, Neptune, and the lamented former planet, Pluto. (These names are from Greco-Roman religion, but are ultimately derived from ancient Babylonian and Assyrian astronomy.)

In the Hebrew Bible—with the notable exception of Genesis 1—the heavenly bodies are also usually regarded as divine beings. One of the astral gods, a rebel called "Shining One, son of Dawn" ("Lucifer" in the Latin translation), attempted to equal God, but instead was cast down into the underworld (Isaiah 14:12–15). This is a story about how one of the astral gods fell from heaven, due to his arrogance and pride. Usually the astral gods are better behaved, serving as God's heavenly courtiers, servants, and militia. According to the book of Job, the morning stars sang praises to God at Creation (Job 38:7), a scene that is conspicuously missing in Genesis. The prophet Micaiah sees the celestial "host of heaven" standing before God (1 Kings 22:19). In the old poem "The Song of Deborah," we see the military aspect of these astral beings: "the stars fought from their (heavenly) paths" against the Canaanite troops (Judges 5:20). Many Israelites seem to worship the heavenly host, which includes the sun and the moon (2 Kings 23:5, Ezekiel 8:16).

In contrast to these shared practices and beliefs, the Creation account in Genesis 1 presents the celestial bodies as purely natural objects, without any divine agency of their own. The common names of the sun and moon—*shemesh* and *yareaḥ*—are avoided, perhaps because these were god-names in Israel and neighboring cultures (for example, the Mesopota-mian sun-god Shamash and the Canaanite moon-god Yariḥ). Instead, Genesis 1 uses the old title, "great lights," to designate these purely natural celestial bodies:

> God made the two great lights—the greater light to rule the day and the lesser light to rule the night—and the stars. And God set them in the vault of heaven to light up the earth, to rule the day and the night, and to separate the light from the darkness. And God saw that it was good. There was evening and there was morning, a fourth day. (Genesis 1:16–19)

The "vault of heaven" is a firm object, a "firmament" (as the Latin translates it), into which God fixed the two great lights and the stars. In Job 27:18, heaven is described as "hard as a mirror of cast metal." The description of the lower heaven as made of jasper stone in the Assyrian text (quoted above) stems from the same shared idea.

In Genesis 1, God creates the celestial bodies so that they will execute three tasks: "to light up the earth, to rule the day and the night, and to separate the light from the darkness" (Genesis 1:17). On the first day of Creation God created light and started the temporal cycle of day and night ("And there was light . . . and there was evening and there was morning, the first day," Genesis 1:5). Now, on the fourth day, God creates the celestial bodies to rule and regulate light and darkness and the procession of time. The celestial bodies are mechanisms that God creates to regulate processes that God has already set into motion.

The picture of the sky and the heavenly bodies in Genesis 1 is not modern science, but it is a model of reality based on observation, and it works well enough. It is a conceptual model that works as "science" in the sense described by W. V. Quine:

> The totality of our so-called knowledge or beliefs, from the most casual matters of geography and history to the profoundest laws of atomic physics or even of pure mathematics and logic, is a man-made fabric which impinges on experience only along the edges. Or, to change the figure, total science is like a field of force whose boundary conditions are experience. A conflict with experience at the periphery occasions readjustments in the interior of the field.[3]

The model of reality in Genesis 1 "impinges on experience only along the edges," where we experience the rhythms of light and darkness, day and night, and where we see the motion of the heavenly bodies against the sky. Genesis 1 also enables us to contemplate our place in the cosmos and our relationships and responsibilities within it. Until the rise of modern science, it was a wholly adequate model. It is ancient science, in the sense of a system of "knowledge" (Latin *scientia*) that explains observable regularities in the world of experience. Only with the discoveries of modern science did there arise an irreconcilable "conflict with experience at the periphery," when Galileo pointed his telescope at the sky.

The cosmos in Genesis 1 is ancient science in another sense: it is an intellectual critique of previous tradition. Where in ancient Israel and neighboring cultures the heavenly bodies were usually seen as gods, in Genesis 1 the celestial bodies are denuded of their divinity. They are not gods, but "great lights." In this naturalizing move, the cosmos is transformed into a purely material, sensible world—as nature—in contrast to God, who transcends nature. This absolute separation between God and nature is a new step in the ancient world. Where previously the heavenly bodies were objects *and* gods—without any formal contradiction between these two properties—now they are *only* natural objects. In Babylonian texts, as Francesca Rochberg explains,

[The god] Sin, in this sense, was the moon and the moon-god. . . . [He] was conceived of as transcending the limits of the physical world, yet was manifested in lunar phenomena. Both notions, the transcendent and the immanent, were expressible.[4]

But in Genesis 1, a clear separation is drawn between the transcendent God and the world of nature. The sun and moon are just natural objects in the firmament. The naturalization of the cosmos in Genesis 1 is comparable to the pre-Socratic cosmologies of the Greek world, which began to be formulated at about the same time as the composition of Genesis 1 (ca. 600 BCE). It is an overstatement to describe this shift as a one-step move from myth to science, but it is an intellectual critique and revision of tradition, and a partial "disenchantment" of the universe.

In Genesis 1, God's words alone create the cosmic order of nature and culture. It is a well-formed but inanimate cosmos, which God creates without conflict or opposition. After his work of Creation, God surveys it and is satisfied: "God saw everything that he made and, behold, it was very good" (Genesis 1:31). He then rests on the seventh day and makes it holy, which provides the reason for his later commandment: "Remember the Sabbath day, to keep it holy" (Exodus 20:8). The cosmos is a complex system, designed by a transcendent Creator. To understand the universe—as we see in Genesis and elsewhere—involves observation and religious observance. It is a celestial science and a theology.

A Handmaid's Tale

Later interpreters of Genesis had two serious chal-
lenges. One was to reconcile the picture of the cosmos
in Genesis 1 with other biblical accounts of Creation,
as in the Garden of Eden story and elsewhere (e.g., Isaiah 40, Psalm 104, Job 38). The other was to reconcile
the resulting picture with works of natural and celestial
science. The second task became necessary beginning
in the Greco-Roman era. As we have seen (chapter 4),
Philo of Alexandria accomplished both of these tasks
by harmonizing Genesis with Platonic cosmology. In
Philo's reading, God first created the invisible world of
ideal forms, and then created the sensible, material
world. This dual creation explains the rationale for the
two Creation accounts in Genesis 1 and 2, and accommodates the dual worlds of Platonic cosmology. By his
figural understanding of Genesis, Philo was able to
solve interpretive problems and to synthesize Greek
philosophy with Genesis.

Philo also promoted Plato's idea that philosophy is
the queen of the sciences. Plato made a distinction
between the "preliminary" sciences—which study the
sensible, material world—and philosophy, which studies the higher world of pure being. Grammar, geometry, and physics were preliminary steps in the education of a philosopher. In his figural interpretation of
Genesis, Philo rediscovers this hierarchy of learning in
the relationship between Abraham's two wives, Sarah

and Hagar. Hagar, the handmaid, is subordinate to the true wife, Sarah. Hence they signify the subordination of the "preliminary" sciences (= Hagar) to philosophy and wisdom (= Sarah):

> the handmaiden of wisdom is the general culture gained through the preliminary sciences of the schools.... grammar, geometry, astronomy, rhetoric, music, and all the other branches of intellectual theory ... are symbolized by Hagar, the handmaid of Sarah.[5]

This figural sense explains why Abraham, who hopes to have children with Sarah, must first have a son with Sarah's handmaid, Hagar. The mind (= Abraham) must first be educated in the preliminary sciences (= Hagar); only then is it ready for philosophy and true wisdom (= Sarah). The union of the mind with higher wisdom is the goal.

Philo's interpretation of the handmaid, Hagar, as a symbol of the preliminary sciences, which are subservient to true knowledge, symbolized by Sarah, gave rise to the widespread notion in Late Antiquity and the Middle Ages that the sciences are the "handmaid of theology." Theology is the "queen of the sciences," since it alone addresses true knowledge and higher reality. Since the sciences pertain to the sensible world, they are theology's handmaid. From the perspective of the dual Platonic world, knowledge of sensible things is just a shadow of the knowledge of the changeless world of pure being. True knowledge attends to the higher world, and to this end contemplates the hidden, perfect, figural senses of Scripture.

Augustine makes abundant use of this hierarchy of knowledge in his interpretations of Genesis. Like Philo, Augustine harmonized Greek philosophy with Genesis through his exposition of the sensible and figural senses of Scripture. Although Augustine usually holds that the plain and figural senses are both present, in cases where science clearly contradicts the plain sense, he often appeals to the figural sense alone. For example, in his commentary *The Literal Meaning of Genesis*, he says that God's first act of creation ("And God said, 'Let there be light,' and there was light") could refer to material *and* spiritual light. However, if reason should disprove "the existence of material light . . . existing before the heavens," then the figural reference to spiritual light is the only true meaning of this passage.[6]

In other words, one should accept *only* the figural sense when the plain sense conflicts with scientific knowledge. Augustine writes, "knowledge . . . acquired by unassailable arguments or proved by the evidence of experience" should guide this decision.[7] The strategy for accommodating science and Scripture is therefore simple: "When [natural scientists] are able, from reliable evidence, to prove some fact of physical science, we shall show that it is not contrary to our Scripture."[8]

The figural sense of Scripture makes this task easy. Whenever science conflicts with the plain sense of Scripture, the true meaning of Scripture is the figural sense. As the handmaid of theology, science provides her with precious guidance, showing where Scripture is speaking only figuratively and protecting her from misinterpretation. Since the truth does not contradict itself, the truth of science cannot contradict the truth of Scripture—the handmaid cannot contradict her mistress. According to Augustine and all premodern interpreters of Genesis, Scripture has nothing to fear from science, since their truths are harmonious.

But what happens when the figural sense is no longer a respectable option? When Luther, Rabelais, and others argue that the figural sense is unnecessary and absurd, and that Genesis is not a Platonic allegory? With the advent of this conflict between the handmaid and her queen, the stage is set for the crisis of confidence that attended the birth of modern science. The inevitable clashes between the Word and the World—which came to a climax in the trial of Galileo—changed the life of Genesis utterly.

It Moves

Copernicus's theory of the heliocentric universe caused little trouble until Galileo became its champion sixty years after Copernicus's death. There are two reasons for the delay. First, Copernicus's treatise is mostly incomprehensible to people who are not mathematicians. Second, unknown to Copernicus, the person who arranged the book's publication, a theologian named Andreas Osiander, inserted an anonymous "Letter to the Reader" explaining that Copernicus was not proposing a real theory. As Robert Westman explains:

> Osiander hoped to save Copernicus from a hostile reception by appealing to the old formula according to which astronomy is distinguished from higher disciplines, like philosophy, in its renunciation of physical truth or even probability. Rather, if it provides "a calculus consistent with the observations, that alone is enough."[9]

Since science is a handmaid to theology, it does not pretend to provide a true description of things. According to Osiander's preface, Copernicus's model is merely a device that solves some mathematical problems, and as such has no empirical content. The anonymous preface carefully states that mathematicians were incapable of stating "anything certain unless it has been divinely revealed to them."

The upshot is that Copernicus's model is just a useful fiction and poses no threat to the academy or the Church. Theology remains the supreme path to revelation and certain knowledge. The lesser sciences are concerned with observations and appearances, all of which are shadows of the truth.

But then an Italian mathematician and inventor, Galileo Galilei, made a powerful telescope, pointed it at the heavens, and concluded from his observations that Copernicus's theory was correct. He published his initial discoveries, describing the orbits of the moons of Jupiter and the phases of Venus as it circles the sun, in *The Starry Messenger* (1610), which made him famous. Along with his fame, Galileo gained new enemies, who criticized his advocacy of the Copernican model as a "real" theory of the universe. Some friends advised him to speak more cautiously and to stay within the bounds of mathematics as a hypothetical science. Galileo, consistent with his view of the realism of scientific inquiry, did not heed this advice.

In 1613 Galileo wrote a letter in which he defended his views against his critics. Since, he argued, Copernicus's theory is demonstrably true, and since truth is indivisible, the heliocentric theory must be in harmony with the Bible. In Galileo's words,

> it being obvious that two truths can never contradict each other, the task of wise interpreters is to strive to find the true meanings of scriptural passages agreeing with those physical conclusions of which we are already certain and sure from clear sensory experience or from necessary demonstrations.[10]

The Bible and science, both being true, must be perfectly harmonious.

Two years later he expanded the letter (which circulated informally—he wisely delayed publishing it for two decades) and addressed it to his admirer, the Grand Duchess Christina. He titled it *New and Old Doctrine of the Most Holy Fathers and Esteemed Theolo-*

gians on Preventing the Reckless Use of the Testimony of the Sacred Scripture in Purely Natural Conclusions That Can Be Established by Sense Experience and Necessary Demonstrations. When published, it was immediately suppressed in Catholic countries and placed on the *Index of Prohibited Books*.

Galileo's vehement defense of Copernicus's theory and his denial that it conflicted with the Bible had the opposite of its intended effect. In 1616 the Catholic Church officially condemned Copernicus's theory, declaring that the proposition that the earth moves around the sun is "false [and] altogether contrary to Holy Scripture."[11] Galileo continued to support the Copernican theory, but couched his support with greater caution.

The Church was correct in its claim that Copernicus's theory is "altogether contrary to Holy Scripture." Genesis 1 and other biblical texts clearly presuppose a geocentric universe. The heavenly bodies, which are set in the solid dome of heaven, revolve in their celestial paths daily around the earth. This picture is described poetically in Ecclesiastes 1:5: "The sun rises and the sun sets, and it rushes back to the place from which it rises." This was the standard view in ancient astronomy, and it easily fits the observable data of the naked eye. But Copernicus's mathematical demonstration that the earth revolves around the sun is correct. In other words, the Church's charge that Copernicus's theory is false and contrary to Scripture is both right and wrong. It's right that Copernicus's theory is contrary to Scripture. But it's wrong that Copernicus's theory is false. This was a problem. Science and Scripture were saying different things.

One year after the publication of his masterpiece, *Dialogue Concerning the Two Chief World Systems, Ptolemaic and Copernican* (1632), the Inquisition tried and convicted Galileo. He was declared to be "vehemently suspected of heresy, namely of having held and believed a doctrine which is false and contrary to the divine and Holy Scripture."[12] He was also found guilty "for interpreting Holy Scripture according to [his] own meaning in response to objections based on Scripture" and for making "various propositions against the authority and true meaning of Holy Scripture."[13]

The second charge refers to Galileo's letters, which had circulated widely among his enemies, in which he had argued for the harmonization of Copernican theory with Scripture. In other words, Galileo's interpretation of Scripture was as much a problem as his scientific work itself. From the testimony of the letters, he was guilty of violating "the authority and true meaning" of Scripture. What were these heretical propositions? In brief, Galileo harmonized Genesis with science by using the method advocated by Augustine: he relied on the figural sense of Scripture.

In his letters, Galileo declares that the problem lies with those who hold to the plain meaning of Scripture:

Though Scripture cannot err, nevertheless some of its interpreters and expositors can sometimes err in various ways. One of these would be very serious and very frequent, namely, to want to limit oneself always to the literal meaning of the words.[14]

In contrast, Galileo appeals to the figural sense, since, as Augustine advocates, one should not be bound to the "literal meaning of the words":

Holy Scripture can never lie, as long as its true meaning has been grasped; but I do not think one can deny that this is frequently obscure and very different from what appears to be the literal meaning of the words. . . . [If] someone were to limit himself always to the pure literal meaning, and if the latter were wrong, then he could make Scripture appear to be full . . . of contradictions and false propositions.[15]

Galileo appeals to the traditional idea of "accommodation"—meaning that the speech of Scripture often accommodates itself to the limited intellect of humans. Where the Holy Spirit speaks in "accommodated" speech, the interpreter must seek the truth from the hidden, cryptic, figural senses:

Since these propositions dictated by the Holy Spirit were expressed by the sacred writers in such a way as to accommodate the capacities of the very unrefined and undisciplined masses, therefore . . . it is necessary that wise interpreters formulate the true meaning.[16]

However, in contrast to Scripture, nature does not accommodate itself to the human intellect: "Nature is inexorable and immutable ... and does not care whether or not her obscure reasons and ways of operating are disclosed to human understanding."[17] The testimony of nature is sure and reliable, and therefore must condition the true interpretation of Scripture. Galileo concludes:

a natural phenomenon which is placed before our eyes by sense experience or proved by necessary demonstration should not be called into question, let alone condemned, on account of scriptural passages whose words appear to have a different meaning.[18]

Galileo's argument is well structured and sensible. It is wholly in line with Augustine's strategy of biblical interpretation. As a pious Catholic, Galileo held that the words of Scripture are true, and as a great scientist he understood the reliability and realism of scientific inquiry. His argument rests, however, on a recently weakened assumption—that Scripture is a cryptic text, whose truth often lies in its hidden senses. This assumption, which no one questioned in Augustine's time, had been severely criticized by Luther and the other reformers, and subsequently by Catholic scholars as well. The official Jesuit educational guide declared that one must interpret Scripture "according to its authentic and literal interpretation."[19] The cryptic sense of Scripture was a broken reed by the time of Galileo.

As Galileo's discoveries illustrate, realism was now ascendant. When he raised his telescope to the sky, he was not looking for an invisible perfect world. He was observing the sensible world, without any regard for a higher Platonic reality. Galileo was an empirical scientist, for whom the sensible world is real, not a shadow of the intelligible world. When he published his drawings of craters on the surface of the moon and the sunspots on the sun, he demonstrated that the celestial objects were not perfect. Conservative academics and theologians were scandalized. Celestial reality is messy, pockmarked, and often catastrophic, not perfect and luminous. Science was about the real universe, which was no longer a shadow. The Platonic duality of worlds and the symbolist mentality of the Middle Ages were buried with the rise of Galilean science.

But Galileo did not realize that the figural interpretation of Scripture was rooted in the figural interpretation of nature. He rejected the figural interpretation of the sensible world, in which science is a lesser branch of learning and studies mere shadows and appearances. He maintained that science is not a convenient fiction, but a rigorous description of the real world. The heliocentric model was correct according to observation and mathematical calculation, and so the plain sense of Scripture must yield to its figural sense. This was the method of Augustine, the towering Church Father. But the mental climate of Augustine's time had come and gone. The figural sense of Scripture wasn't easily available any more. The Reformation, the new learning, and Rabelaisian laughter had seen to that. Galileo was clutching at what other scholars and theologians—including his Inquisitors—saw as a wax nose.

One of Galileo's critics, Lodovico delle Colombe, makes this point clear. He railed against Galileo: "All theologians without a single exception say that when Scripture can be understood according to the literal sense, it must never be interpreted in any other way."[20] This is basically Luther's position, which a century later was now standard for Protestant *and* Catholic theologians. Galileo's recourse to the hidden sense of Scripture was now grounds for heresy—particularly since the Church had already proclaimed (in its 1616 ruling against Copernican theory) that the plain (geocentric) meaning of Scripture was true. In the judgment of the Inquisition, Galileo had offended against the "the authority and true meaning of Holy Scripture." This also meant that he offended against the authority of the Church to determine the true meaning of Scripture. Because of its allegiance to the plain sense of Genesis 1 and related texts, Galileo's Augustinian argument was rejected.

In his *Letter to the Duchess Christina*, Galileo quoted a cardinal's remark that "the intention of the Holy Spirit is to teach us how one goes to heaven and not how heaven goes."[21] In the spirit of this remark, Galileo wanted to draw a sharp line between the findings of science and the legitimate interests of the Church. But the Inquisition declared that the plain sense of Scripture teaches both how one goes to heaven *and* how heaven goes. It is simultaneously a theology and a celestial science. The Inquisition was right in its estimation of the plain sense of Scripture, but Galileo was right in his view of the real world. The earth does move around the sun.

Galileo was a great scientist, but his way of interpreting Scripture was no longer tenable. His theology was a century out of date. With the figural sense of the world and the Word in decline, the plain sense of Scripture was now on its own, face to face with modern science. The Inquisition prevailed in this first skirmish, but it was a Pyrrhic victory. Galileo became a martyred hero of science, and the authority of the Catholic Church eroded in matters of worldly knowledge.

The Inquisition's verdict instructed Galileo to "abjure, curse, and detest the above-mentioned errors and heresies" or be executed. A proud but practical man, Galileo chose the first option. According to later legend, Galileo left the trial chamber muttering, "Still, it moves" ("*Eppur si muove*"), repudiating the verdict and his recantation. He probably never said these words. Yet the legend is apt—for as Galileo knew, the earth still moves.

Nearly two hundred years after the trial, the Church removed Galileo's and Copernicus's books from the new edition of the *Index of Prohibited Books* (1832). More recently Pope John Paul II rehabilitated Galileo and endorsed his position on the relationship between science and the Bible. In 1992 he declared, echoing Galileo, "the Bible does not concern itself with the details of the physical world." Science is not a handmaid of theology, but a parallel mode of knowledge: "There exist two realms of knowledge, one which has its source in revelation and one which reason can discover by its own power."[22] The autonomy of science is no longer under vehement suspicion of heresy. However, it is a question whether the pope's strategy for harmonizing the Bible and science is any more tenable today than it was in Galileo's day.

After Galileo's trial, the study of nature and Scripture began to diverge. Genesis came increasingly to be seen as an ancient book, written in a foreign language by people whose ideas differed in some respects from modern notions. The antiquity of Genesis began to be visible. Science, in contrast, was written in the language of mathematics, and was concerned with the unchanging laws of nature. The old relationship between the queen and her handmaid began to unravel.

Naturalizing Scripture

After Galileo, science became professionalized. He was the last modern scientist whose scientific writings were meant for a popular audience. In contrast, Isaac Newton's masterpiece, written a half century later, *Philoso-phiae Naturalis Principia Mathematica* (*The Mathe-matical Principles of Natural Philosophy*, 1687) was —and remains—utterly inaccessible to nonspecialists. Science became a technical discipline, as it remains to this day. Similarly, biblical interpretation became more specialized, more focused on the original languages and the Bible's historical circumstances. As the profes-sions of science and biblical criticism began to diverge, their methods—based on empirical evidence, criti-cism, and philosophical realism—began to converge.

The person who invented the procedures of modern biblical scholarship was another heretic, the Dutch Jew Baruch Spinoza. Spinoza was deeply influenced by Galileo's work, particularly by his demonstration of scientific method. Spinoza was a professional lens grinder, whose precision scientific lenses were used in telescopes and other instruments. His choice of profes-sion and his interest in optics were tributes to Galileo. So was his revolutionary approach to the interpreta-tion of the Bible.

Spinoza's *Theological-Political Treatise* (1670), in which he presents his new method of biblical interpre-tation, is, as Jonathan Israel writes, "one of the most profoundly influential philosophical texts in the his-tory of Western thought."[23] It changed the life of Gen-esis and the Bible in ways that we are still trying to comprehend, and continues to shock, delight, and in-furiate. Spinoza took a simple but profound step—he turned Galileo's scientific method toward the Bible.

The difference between the book of nature and the book of Scripture, which Galileo's science announced, turned into a convergence in the method for studying them.

Spinoza argues that the abuse of biblical authority by theologians and civic leaders corrupts both religion and the state, and that a clear formulation of the method of biblical interpretation is a means to counteract these misuses of the Bible. By clarifying the proper method for biblical interpretation, Spinoza clears the way for his advocacy of freedom of speech, freedom of religion, and democracy. The appeal to the Bible by unsavory demagogues has been an obstacle for each of these aims. This is no ivory tower philosophy; rather it is politically and morally charged.

Spinoza diagnoses the underlying problems as human vice and credulity:

> Vice and ambition have in the end exercised so much influence that religion has been made to consist in defending purely human delusions. . . . To extricate ourselves from such confusion and to free our minds from theological prejudices and the blind acceptance of human fictions as God's teaching, we need to analyse and discuss the true method of interpreting Scripture.[24]

Spinoza boldly claims that the scientific method that Galileo successfully used to interpret nature is also the true method for interpreting Scripture:

To formulate the matter succinctly, I hold that the method of interpreting Scripture does not differ from the [correct] method of interpreting nature, but rather is wholly consonant with it.[25]

Now of course Scripture is not nature. As Galileo observed, the book of nature is "written in mathematical language,"[26] while Scripture is written in Hebrew, Aramaic, and Greek. But a rational method of studying Scripture can be consonant with the scientific study of nature. The Bible, like a leaf or a star, is susceptible to careful observation and analysis. But how does one do this? What are the instruments and the relevant data? Spinoza invokes—or perhaps better, invents—a distinctively modern concept of history as the relevant context of interpretation:

> To interpret Scripture, we need to assemble a genuine history of it and to deduce the thinking of the Bible's authors by valid inferences from this history. . . . Provided we admit no other criteria or data for interpreting Scripture and discussing its contents than what is drawn from Scripture itself and its history, we will always proceed without any danger of going astray.[27]

Spinoza's concept of "history" includes what we would call cultural and political history, conceptual worldview, authorial intention, and linguistic and textual history—all without appeal to miracles or divine intervention. Just as Galileo does not invoke God's agency as an "extra" cause in the mathematical laws of motion, so Spinoza sees no need to invoke God as a supplementary cause in human history. Natural and human causes are sufficient for the study of history. In other words, the history and interpretation of Scripture have been naturalized.

Spinoza's view of history sharply diverges from the biblical view. He proposes to view the Bible's history from an analytic, scholarly point of view, not based on Jewish or Christian assumptions. Spinoza's concept of scientific rationality and his personal experience as an outsider—he was banned from the Dutch Jewish community for his heretical views—contribute to his ability to stand outside of the traditional categories of biblical interpretation. His instrument is reason, not tradition or special revelation, nor a confection of all three.

Spinoza's quest for objectivity may be impossible to achieve completely, but it is an essential principle of the scientific method. The ideal for Spinoza was mathematical precision, as it was for Plato and Galileo. But in historical inquiry, as Spinoza observes, "it happens very rarely that men report something straightforwardly, just as it occurred, without intruding any judgment of their own." And philosophers and historians must be "very much on their guard against their own preconceived opinions."[28] In other words, objectivity is a goal, but in some respects an elusive one. This is, of course, a problem for reason, compared to the method of inspiration by the Holy Spirit.

The assumption that Scripture is divine (see chapter 2) is not a part of Spinoza's method. He argues that such a claim should be derived from the careful study of Scripture, not assumed from the outset. Bracketing this traditional assumption allows Spinoza to make another crucial distinction that is characteristically modern—between the "sense of a text" and the "truth of things." In a critical analysis of Scripture, one does not presume that everything that the plain sense means is necessarily true.

> In order not to confuse the genuine sense of a passage with the truth of things, we must investigate a passage's sense only from its use of the language or from reasoning which accepts no other foundation than Scripture itself.[29]

Only in this way—by distinguishing the text's "genuine sense" from the "truth of things"—can we determine what Scripture really means. One must be able to entertain the possibility that a passage's meaning is not true—in a historical, scientific, philosophical, or moral sense. The genuine sense of "And God said, 'Let there be light'" (Genesis 1:3) may not be a true account of the origin of light. Scriptural meaning is not necessarily the same as the truth of things in the real world. This is a dramatic break from the old assumptions about biblical interpretation and the harmony between nature and Scripture. As the Gershwin lyric says, "The things you are liable to read in the Bible, It ain't necessarily so."

By making this distinction Spinoza opens an intellectual space for modern biblical criticism. Henceforth a scholar's religious and philosophical commitments are irrelevant—or even an obstacle—to the task of biblical interpretation. As a scholar one tries to discover the religious and philosophical commitments of the biblical text, and not make it parrot one's own views. This is a difficult task, requiring the self-conscious effort, but it is necessary in order to hear the genuine voice of a passage.

Spinoza's retooling of Galileo's scientific method is the invention of the "historical-critical method." Empirical, rational, systematic inquiry is turned from the interpretation of nature to the interpretation of Scripture. It is scandalous, revolutionary, and—in retrospect—clearly necessary in the modern world. The Bible is amenable to rational inquiry, just as is the movement of the earth around the sun.

The ancestry of this method is, of course, not limited to Galileo. Luther is a key influence, although he would not be pleased by it. Spinoza's categories are, in several respects, refinements of Luther's. Spinoza relies on "reasoning which accepts no other foundation than Scripture itself." This is a retooling of Luther's doctrine of *sola scriptura*, "Scripture alone," in which the clear words of Scripture are the sole foundation—not tradition, the Church, or other human authorities. In his speech to the Diet of Worms, Luther appealed to the "testimony of Scripture" and "clear reason" as his authorities. With a twist of emphasis, Spinoza appeals to the same authorities. But where Luther supplements reason with the inspiration of the Holy Spirit, Spinoza is content with reason alone.

The implications of this new method for the life of Genesis are far-reaching. Spinoza points out the historical context of the passage that states, when Abraham entered the Promised Land, "The Canaanites were then in the land" (Genesis 12:6). The medieval commentator Ibn Ezra had written, "There is a secret meaning to the text. Let the one who understands it remain silent."[30] Spinoza, ignoring Ibn Ezra's advice, points out that the historical location of the writer of this passage must be a time when there were no more Canaanites in the land:

> The text excludes the present time, i.e. the time of
> the writer, which is not therefore the time of
> Moses, because in his time [the Canaanites] still
> possessed that territory. This is the mystery about
> which Ibn Ezra recommends silence.[31]

This passage—and many others that Spinoza cites— indicates that the Pentateuch was composed in the land of Israel long after the time of Moses. He famously concludes, "From all this it is plainer than the noonday sun that the Pentateuch was not written by Moses but by someone else who lived many generations after Moses."[32]

Spinoza points out a number of internal contradictions among the stories of Genesis, which indicate that the book was not written in one go. He argues that an editor—perhaps Ezra the Scribe—"made no final version . . . but merely collected narratives from different writers."[33] For instance, according to the internal chronology of the book, Jacob must have been eighty-four years old when he married Leah and Rachel (Genesis 30); Dinah was seven years old when she was raped by Shechem (Genesis 34:1–4); and Simeon and Levi were twelve and eleven years old, respectively, when they killed Shechem and all the men of his city (Genesis 34:25–26). These ages, derived from the sequence of stories, seem absurd. He concludes:

> We have only to notice that everything in these five books, commandments and histories alike, is narrated in a confused manner, without order and without respect for chronology, and that stories are repeated, sometimes in different versions. We will then easily see that they were all collected and stored away.[34]

In the centuries since Spinoza, biblical scholars have expended massive effort and ingenuity to untangle these discrepancies, yielding the model of the authorship of the Pentateuch that we call the "documentary hypothesis," with its alphabet soup of J, E, P, D, and other smaller source texts.

Finally, Spinoza argues that "theology is not subordinate to reason nor reason to theology," but that each has its own domain. Neither one is a handmaid of the other.

CHAPTER 6

Religion and piety should not wish to have reason for a servant nor should reason wish to have religion for a servant. Both should be able to rule their own realms in the greatest harmony.[35]

Because of their independence, there is no cause to accommodate Scripture to science, or to subordinate science to Scripture. Spinoza concludes that "neither is subordinate to the other; each has its own kingdom."[36]

The truce that Spinoza called between religion and reason has had a checkered history. But Spinoza's ideals of freedom of speech, freedom of religion, and liberal democracy have certainly taken root in the modern world. In many cases religion and science have learned how to coexist. After all, Pope John Paul II agreed with Galileo's position on the relationship between science and Scripture. And Einstein agreed with Spinoza's position on the nature of God—he said, "my God is the God of Spinoza." We might all agree that Genesis contains important and consequential meanings, even if its cosmology differs from "the truth of things."

Spinoza's prescription for the interpretation of Scripture in the light of reason and history took root slowly. His book was roundly attacked and immediately placed on the *Index of Prohibited Books*. Most of his readers viewed Spinoza as a notorious heretic— which contributed to making the *Treatise* an underground best-seller. But scholars gradually adopted his method. A Catholic priest, Richard Simon, wrote an erudite *Critical History of the Old Testament* (1685) to refute Spinoza's conclusions, but adopted Spinoza's method to do it. He wrote in a letter to a colleague:

> It is right and proper to condemn the impious conclusions which Spinoza draws from some of the axioms he lays down; but those axioms are not always false in themselves, not always to be cast aside.[37]

With this new method and the erudition of Simon and the parade of scholars that followed, modern biblical criticism had come to stay.

The New World and the Old Earth

The wider world was changing in the era when Galileo and Spinoza published their revolutionary views about nature and Scripture. The world was getting bigger and older, and the place of Genesis in world history was getting complicated. Two key discoveries in early modern times were particularly important in changing the life of Genesis: the lands and peoples of the New World, and the antiquity of the earth. Each of these had wide-ranging repercussions on the interpretation of Genesis.

The discovery of the New World changed people's consciousness about the diversity of human civilizations and the complexity of history. Since Genesis was the standard model of world history, and the "Table of Nations" in Genesis 10 was the canonical list of peoples, the discovery of the New World raised challenging questions. Suddenly there were peoples and lands that Genesis didn't seem to know about. Many efforts were made to accommodate the genealogies of Genesis to the peoples of the New World.

This was a lively debate during the sixteenth and seventeenth centuries, when the New World was being intensively explored and colonized.[38] Sometimes connections were based on imaginative etymologies. For example, Benito Arias Montano argued that Yoktan, son of Eber (Genesis 10:25), had given his name to the Yucatan peninsula of Mexico. But Sir Walter Raleigh pointed out that the natives didn't call their land Yucatan—the name was a mistake by the Spanish explorers.[39] So much for this theory. A French explorer, Marc Lescarbot, proposed that Noah was born in the New World and resettled it after the Flood. No one was persuaded. Spinoza's own teacher, Manasseh Ben Israel, revived the theory that the people of the New World were descendants of the lost Ten Tribes of Israel. Oliver Cromwell, intrigued by the apocalyptic implications of this theory, invited Ben Israel to England and shortly after allowed Jews to resettle in England. Such are the consequences of theories about the Jewish Indians.

The sheer number and variety of theories eroded their plausibility. The Italian scholar Giordano Bruno argued for a separate origin of the peoples of the New World, for which—among other heresies—he was burned at the stake in 1600. Fifty years later, Isaac La Peyrère published a scandalous book, *Men Before*

Adam, and barely escaped the fire. He argued that the ancestors of the peoples of Mexico, China, and other distant lands were products "of the first and most ancient creation ... and not propagated with Adam."[40] Since Genesis does not list these people, they must have had a separate creation. This is an ingenious theory, but it presumes that Genesis is flawed and incomplete. La Peyrère's book was placed on the *Index of Prohibited Books*, and he was forced to recant.

The Lost Tribes theory had the most staying power. It was popular in England and in the American colonies. The founder of Pennsylvania, William Penn, wrote of the Native Americans: "As to the original of this extraordinary people, I cannot but believe they are of the Jewish race, I mean of the stock of the ten tribes so long lost."[41] This theory remained popular into the nineteenth century, and a version of it is enshrined in *The Book of Mormon*, according to which Native Americans are descended from the tribe of Manasseh.

But by the mid-nineteenth century, these theories were largely discredited because there was no evidence for them. While most people assumed that everyone descended from Noah, the genealogies of Genesis seemed at best vague about the specifics. Many historians concluded that Genesis only knew about the Old World, not the New. The genealogies of Genesis no longer seemed to correspond to the "truth of things" in the wider world. As Mark Twain quipped, "There is one very impressive thing about the Deity of the Bible, and that is his lack of information. He did not know there was an America; he did not know that the globe was round."[42] In the eyes of many, it seemed that the world was larger than the one described in Genesis.

The world was also getting older. The modern study of geology began during Spinoza's lifetime, when a Danish geologist, Nicolas Steno, made important discoveries about the strata of geological formations and the nature of fossils. Steno, a pious man who became a Catholic bishop, was content to fit his discoveries into the biblical chronology. The major breakthrough occurred a century later with the researches of James Hutton, whose book *Theory of the Earth* (1788) first showed the vast scale of geological time. Hutton discovered that "our fertile plains are formed from the ruins of mountains" and our continents from the bottom of ancient oceans. With the slow and massive cycling of rocks, Hutton discovered the astonishing antiquity of the earth. He memorably wrote, "That Time, which measures every thing in our idea, and is often deficient to our schemes, is to nature endless and as nothing."[43] Geologists call this the discovery of "deep time."

But Genesis places the origin of the universe at approximately 6,000 years ago. (Archbishop Ussher famously dated the first day of Creation to Sunday, October 23, 4004 BCE.) How could the earth actually be millions of years old? After the implications of Hutton's discovery became clear to other geologists, attempts were made to harmonize "deep time" with Genesis. Two strategies that became popular in the early nineteenth century were the "day-age theory" and the "gap theory." Both were naturalized versions of older figural interpretations.

In his *Introduction to Geology* (1813), Robert Bakewell argued that a "day" in Genesis 1 is not a literal day, and so can refer to a vast period of time. He writes, "The six days in which Creative Energy renovated the globe and called into existence the different classes of animals, will imply six successive epochs of indefinite duration." Hence he "reconcile[s] . . . the epochs of creation with the six days mentioned by Moses."[44] Bakewell was not a conservative theologian but a practicing geologist. His reconciliation of Genesis and geology followed the commonplace view that there can be no conflict between the two.

Bakewell's appeal to a nonliteral meaning of the word "day" has the precedent of earlier interpreters such as Augustine, who accommodated Genesis to contemporary science by reading "day" in a figural sense. Since Augustine followed Plato (*Timaeus*) in believing that the creation of all things must have happened simultaneously , Augustine reads "day" as signifying "the light of wisdom" or "angelic knowledge."[45] Augustine empties the word "day" of its temporal meaning in order to harmonize Genesis with Plato. Bakewell uses the same strategy, but the figural sense now becomes a harmonization with nature. In order to accommodate Genesis to geology, Bakewell expands the temporal meaning of "day" indefinitely.

Another popular harmonization was the "gap theory." This was first proposed by the Scottish mathematician Thomas Chalmers in his treatise *On the Miraculous and Internal Evidences of the Christian Revelation* (1814). Chalmers argued for a large gap of time between the first verse of Genesis—"In the beginning God created the heavens and the earth"—and the six days of creation. With the insertion of eons of time after the first verse—by recent count, 4.5 billion years—the geological age of the earth is "hidden" in Genesis.

Early interpreters such as Philo and Augustine had posited two Creations—of the intelligible and material worlds—based on the repetitions in Genesis 1 and 2. Chalmers's appeal to a temporal "gap" between the verses violates the grammar of the Hebrew text, but is a normal strategy in figural interpretation. This "naturalizing" of the figural sense is a curious move—with one foot in premodern interpretation and the other foot in modern science. Yet such harmonizing maneuvers seemed unproblematic to many scholars of the time, for whom the bond between the Bible and science was still secure.

As with the awareness of the New World, the discovery of the old earth came to be accepted as common knowledge. The world was now vastly older than people had known previously. As Paolo Rossi observes, this was a serious change in outlook:

Men in [the late seventeenth century] had a past of six thousand years; those of [the late eighteenth century] were conscious of a past of millions of years. The difference lies not only between living at the center or at the margins of the universe, but also between living in a present relatively close to the origins (and having at hand, what is more, a text that narrates the *entire* history of the world) or living instead in a present behind which stretches the "dark abyss" . . . of an almost infinite time.[46]

The Genesis texts that narrates the early history of the world had to be stretched to fit the real world, or the lack of fit would cause a break between Genesis and the world. By the late eighteenth century, many people—and most biblical scholars—came to view the early stories of Genesis as ancient fables or myths. But there was still room for believers to assume that science and Scripture could be harmonized—with gaps, day-ages, or other devices. For both camps, the New World and the old earth became accepted facts. The different reactions to modern knowledge reached a delicate equilibrium: on one side, those with doubts about the agreement of Genesis and science, and on the other, those who believed that, with small adjustments, Genesis and science could still be harmonized.

The Breaking Point

Two events in the mid-nineteenth century—in 1859 and 1860—upended this delicate equilibrium. First, Charles Darwin published *On the Origin of Species*, which seemed to demonstrate that all forms of life evolved by purely natural processes. Divine agency was nowhere to be found. In one sentence, Darwin hinted at what everyone understood: "light will be thrown on the origin of man and his history."[47] Darwinian evolution by natural selection could not be harmonized with Genesis 1, in which God creates all the kinds of birds, fish, and land animals in two days, much less his creation of humans "in the image of God." Nor could it be harmonized with Genesis 2, in which God creates man first, then animals, and finally woman. Biology now had its own "deep time," during which species evolved, competed for resources, and became extinct. None of this was known in Genesis.

Bishop Samuel Wilberforce of Oxford—known to his detractors as "Soapy Sam" because of his slippery arguments—wrote a scathing review of Darwin's book:

> Man's derived supremacy over the earth . . . man's fall and man's redemption; the incarnation of the Eternal Son; the indwelling of the Eternal Spirit,— all are equally and utterly irreconcilable with the degrading notion of the brute origin of him who was created in the image of God.[48]

If people descended from other species, then Genesis—and with it, biblical religion itself—was simply wrong. Science and religion could no longer be accommodated. For Wilberforce and his conservative allies, the gloves came off. Darwin's theory of evolution was sheer heresy.

But things got worse. Four months after the appearance of the *On the Origin of Species*, another book appeared with the innocuous name *Essays and Reviews*. Written by seven Oxford scholars, six of whom were clergymen of the Church of England, the essays summarized the latest findings of biblical scholarship to ordinary churchgoing readers. The public was stunned.

In his essay on "Mosaic Cosmogony," Charles Goodwin argues that Genesis 1 is not scientifically accurate, but that it should not be despised on that account or distorted to fit with science. It has value of a different kind, as an ancient work of genius:

> If we regard it as the speculation of some Hebrew
> Descartes or Newton, promulgated in all good
> faith as the best and most probable account that
> could be then given of God's universe, it resumes
> the dignity and value of which the writers in ques-
> tion have done their utmost to deprive it.[49]

As for Adam and Eve, essayist Henry Wilson allows that the Garden of Eden story is unhistorical, but that it nonetheless asserts a "great moral truth":

> Some may consider the descent of all mankind
> from Adam and Eve as an undoubted historical
> fact; others may rather perceive in that relation a
> form of narrative into which in early ages tradition
> would easily throw itself spontaneously.... [The
> story] became the concrete expression of a great

moral truth—of the brotherhood of all human beings, of their community, as in other things so also
in suffering and in frailty, in physical pains and
moral "corruption." And the force, grandeur and
reality of these ideas are not a whit impaired.[50]

These represent the standard view at the time
in German biblical scholarship, derived from J. G.
Herder, who assimilated Spinoza's method to a romantic sensibility. Genesis might be scientifically inaccu-
rate, but it was noble in its antiquity and truthful in its
morality. It was, in Herder's view, the oldest and purest
poetry of humankind:

> If you read through the Bible with a humane eye
> and heart, if you also follow the thread of God's
> development according to times, life-styles, people,
> and morals, then what truth you will find, and
> with all that is miraculous in many a story, what
> powerful truth![51]

This new romantic sensibility regarding the Bible was
shocking to the English public. The fact that such
views were being advanced by Christian clergy, and not
by eccentric freethinkers, created a scandal. *Essays and
Reviews* sold over 20,000 copies in two years, more
than Darwin's *Origin* sold in twenty years.

"Soapy Sam" Wilberforce was up in arms. In a scathing review he called for the expulsion of the authors
from the Church of England, and warned those of im-

pressionable mind to avoid the book's seductive evils. He argued forcefully that even a modernized Christianity must hold onto some objective truths:

> All unbelievers of all classes, and all believers of all shades, see plainly enough that the essayists are simply deceiving themselves in their impossible attempt to surrender all the objective truths of Christianity and yet to retain its subjective powers.[52]

Can Christianity surrender the factuality of Genesis and retain its redemptive purpose? This is a difficult question. Can the Bible, as Kierkegaard had recently argued, be objectively false but subjectively true?[53] Wilberforce had no doubts on this score. He brought charges of "erroneous, strange and heretical doctrines" against two of the authors, and the Church court condemned them. After further controversy, the Church of England formally condemned *Essays and Reviews*. One wag attacked the essays as "Each one a dull libel / 'Gainst plain sense and the Bible."[54] Sales of the book soared, and the battle lines between Christian liberals and conservatives hardened.

The Fundamentals

The twin threats of biblical scholarship and evolution had an even greater effect in America, striking the first sparks of fundamentalism. A few years after Darwin published his scandalous sequel, *The Descent of Man, and Selection in Relation to Sex* (1871), a group of Protestant evangelicals at a "Believers' Meeting for Bible Study" produced a fourteen-point creed (later called the Niagara Creed) that gave birth to fundamentalism as a modern movement. The preamble to the creed diagnoses the problem:

> So many in the latter times have departed from the faith, giving heed to seducing spirits, and doctrines, of devils; so many have turned away their ears from the truth, and turned into fables; so many are busily engaged in scattering broadcast the seeds of fatal error . . . we are constrained by fidelity to Him to make the following declaration of our doctrinal belief.[55]

The first point of the creed is an affirmation of the inspiration of every detail of Scripture "to the smallest word":

> We believe . . . that the Holy Ghost gave the very words of the sacred writings to holy men of old; and that His Divine inspiration is not in different degrees, but extends equally and fully to all parts of these writings, historical, poetical, doctrinal and prophetical, and to the smallest word, and inflection of a word.[56]

This is an affirmation of the uniform inspiration and inerrancy of every word and grammatical detail in the original Scriptures. Prior to this creed, no one had gone so far in privileging the plain sense of Scripture. Luther was not bothered by the occasional errors in Scripture, nor was Calvin or the other Reformers. Luther's distinction between law and gospel made it clear that he regarded the Holy Ghost's inspiration as unevenly distributed in Scripture. Earlier theologians—both Christian and Jewish—had found divine inspiration in the hidden figural meanings of Scripture as much as in its plain sense. But now the Holy Ghost's inspiration concerned the plain meanings of Scripture and "extends equally and fully to all parts," down to the smallest details. And now the inerrancy of the plain sense became a sacred belief, drawing a theological boundary that must not be crossed.

After the erosion of the cryptic senses of Scripture, the truth of the plain sense was now under threat by scientists and biblical scholars. Conservatives took shelter in an uncompromising doctrine of the total inspiration and inerrancy of the Bible. The new doctrinal statements were strongly influenced by a group of conservative theologians from Princeton Seminary, who formed the brain trust of early fundamentalism.

Princeton theologians A. A. Hodge and Benjamin B. Warfield published a full account of the new doctrine of biblical inerrancy in an article on "Inspiration" in the *Presbyterian Review* of 1881. They refined the Niagara Creed statement as follows:

All the affirmations of Scripture of all kinds
whether of spiritual doctrine or duty, or of physical

or historical fact, or of psychological or philosophical principle, are without any error, when the *ipsissima verba* of the original autographs are ascertained and interpreted in their natural and intended sense.[57]

This position—which is authoritative in fundamentalist circles to this day—has some interesting strategic features. It accepts the validity of interpreting the words of Scripture "in their natural and intended sense." The plain sense alone is authoritative. But where the findings of science or scholarship conflict with the plain sense of Scripture, it finds authority in a literal sense *that is now hidden*. Inerrancy is a property of a partially lost Scripture—"the original autographs." In other words, the Bible of today may differ from the original dictation of the Holy Spirit. Where it conflicts with science or scholarship, the fundamentalist can claim that the manuscripts of the original Bible said something different.

The cryptic sense of Scripture is revived in this argument, but it has been historicized. The hidden meanings are located in the (no longer existing) original copies of the Bible, which were corrupted in the course of their textual transmission. The apparent errors in Scripture are due to the mistakes or alterations of ancient scribes. The true meaning is hidden—lost in the historical past—but present at the original moment of revelation. This is a breathtaking revision of the old assumption of the cryptic sense of Scripture. The cryptic sense is now the original literal sense, but it is now hidden in the sands of time. The true words of Scripture are not open to criticism, because they may no longer exist in the material world.

If one wanted to contest the statements in Genesis, "And God said, 'Let there be a firmament in the midst of the waters,'" or "[Lot's] wife looked behind and turned into a pillar of salt" (Genesis 1:6; 19:26), according to this doctrine one would first have to prove that they are in the original text of Genesis. Hodge and Warfield write, "Let it be proved that each alleged discrepant statement certainly occurred in the original autograph of the sacred book."[58] But this cannot be done, because the original manuscript no longer exists. As an evangelical scholar recently commented, these conditions "completely guarantee that no error could ever be charged against the Bible."[59] The new hidden sense of Scripture, lodged in the historical past, provides a shield against the prying eyes of science and scholarship.

According to this argument, there is no conflict between Genesis and science—nor are there internal inconsistencies in Genesis—since no error can be proved in the original words, which are no longer accessible. In cases of apparent discrepancy, the truth is hidden. As Hodge and Warfield contend:

> There is no real conflict between the really ascertained facts of science and the first two chapters of Genesis rightly interpreted, [which] of itself dem-

onstrates that a supernatural intelligence must have directed the writing of those chapters. This, of course, proves that the scientific element of Scripture, as well as the doctrinal, was within the scope of Inspiration.[60]

No error can be proved because the Inspired Word is only in the "original autograph" of Scripture, which we no longer have. This is a masterful argument, which precludes any proof of biblical error. However, it is also a self-defeating argument, because it also precludes any consistent reliance on what Luther called "the clear words of Scripture." It regards the Bible that we read as an incorrigibly corrupted text, unreliable in its details, unstable in its support of any particular interpretation of its meanings, because its true words are hidden. The plain sense is now a bruised reed, which does not bear weight.

Charles Briggs, a biblical scholar and coeditor of the *Presbyterian Review*, was highly critical of this new doctrine. In his theological manifesto *Whither?* (1889), he maintained that Hodge and Warfield had constructed "a new theory of the inerrancy of Scripture. . . . Such a position is a serious and hazardous departure from Protestant orthodoxy."[61] He described their position as "theological rubbish."[62] But Briggs's moderate views were drowned out, and he was charged and convicted of heresy by the Presbyterian Church. The conservatives wholly embraced the doctrine of inerrancy formulated by Hodge and Warfield, which remains the gold standard for Christian fundamentalists and evangelicals.

The word "fundamentalist" was inspired by the publication in 1910–15 of a set of twelve paperback volumes called *The Fundamentals: A Testimony to the Truth*.[63] This work, an American reaction to the liberal vision embodied in *Essays and Reviews*, was the brainchild of two wealthy California oilmen, who distributed some three million free volumes.

Many of the essays in *The Fundamentals* contain attacks on biblical scholarship or evolution. An essay called "My Personal Experience with the Higher Criticism," by J. J. Reeve, a professor from Southwestern Theological Seminary, gives a sense of the tone of the essays, which is often quite calm and reasonable. Reeve tells how he was almost seduced by modern scholarship but narrowly escaped from its false worldview:

> It is their philosophy or world-view that is responsible for all their speculations and theories. Their mental attitude towards the world and its phenomena is the same as their attitude toward the Bible.... [U]pon closer thinking I saw that the whole movement with its conclusions was the result of the adoption of the hypothesis of evolution.... This worldview is wonderfully fascinating and almost compelling.... But more careful consideration convinced me that the little truth in it served to sugar-coat and give plausibility to some deadly errors that lurked within.[64]

Reeve's personal story is moving, as he senses the allure of false idols and successfully resists temptation. In the end he sees through this "cultured and refined heathenism with a Christian veneer"[65] and embraces what he believes to be biblical Christianity.

Reeve rightly connects the naturalism of modern biblical scholarship with the naturalism of science. For this he blames Darwin rather than Galileo and Spinoza. His historical argument is wrong, but he rightly senses the tension between scientific reason and the plain sense of Scripture. How can Christianity abandon worldly knowledge to science, if the clear words of Scripture are about the world?

With no Platonic world to fall back on and no figural meaning to decipher, the plain sense of Scripture alone faces the realism of science and scholarship. The conflicting worldviews—supernaturalism versus naturalism and faith versus reason—call for a choice. For the fundamentalist, the choice is clear. As Reeve puts it, one can stand with "a partial and one-sided intellectualism" or with "the fundamental tenets of Biblical Christianity."[66] In this contest, the hollow claims of reason are no match for the holy fundamentals. But we may question whether the conflict is quite as stark—with only two choices—as the one framed by Reeve. There may be more nuanced responses to the crisis of modernity.

The affirmation of biblical inerrancy turns into a fiery sermon in the essay on "The Bible and Modern

Criticism" by Frédéric Bettex, a Swiss evangelical scholar:

> Let us then, by repudiating this modern criticism, show our condemnation of it. What does it offer us? Nothing. What does it take away? Everything. Do we have any use for it? No! It neither helps us in life nor comforts us in death; it will not judge us in the world to come.[67]

Modern scholarship is repudiated as a thing made by man, which is worthless compared to the things made by God, including every word of Genesis and Holy Scripture. The fundamentalist line has been drawn.

Jerry Falwell used to say that "a fundamentalist is an evangelical who is angry about something."[68] Modern fundamentalism arose out of anger at science (mostly evolution) and biblical scholarship. Fundamentalists are angry about other things too, but these are the fundamental problems. Although modern fundamentalists often think that theirs is the authentic old-time religion, its lineage barely goes back a hundred years. Fundamentalism was born in the Gilded Age of America, and is a movement of conservative populism and nostalgia—and a hunger for the truth of the Bible's plain sense. Its affirmation of simple truths and its distrust of intellectual elites strike deep chords in the American psyche.

As George Marsden writes, fundamentalism "is antimodernist, but in some respects strikingly modern."[69] Genesis is treated "as though it were a scientific treatise

... essentially a collection of true and precise propositions."[70] Fundamentalism was born when the life of Genesis became too complicated, when it seemed that science and scholarship were tying it in knots and emptying it of truth. But fundamentalism makes Genesis compatible with science at a high price, by hiding its true meanings in a lost world of original autographs, and by exalting its convoluted doctrine as queen, to which science and scholarship must bow.

The life of Genesis began a new phase—a long midlife crisis—when it encountered modern science and biblical scholarship. Old assumptions were questioned, and new problems, which had previously been unthinkable, became unavoidable. With the combined impact of Darwinian evolution and the new school of biblical criticism, the long-lived goal of harmonization came to a halt. The result was a polarization between a modern Genesis and a fundamentalist Genesis, with accusations of heresy on both sides.

The parting of the ways represented by our two controversial essay collections—liberal Christianity in *Essays and Reviews* and fundamentalism in *The Fundamentals*—does not exhaust the range of responses to the crisis of modernity in the life of Genesis. We now turn to other responses, which are often more subtle and disturbing. Some writers, politicians, revolutionaries, and scholars saw new possibilities beyond the tug-of-war between modernists and fundamentalists over Genesis. What they created out of this crisis is the subject of our final chapter.

Modern Times

CHAPTER 7

"He threw himself onto his bed and took from the
nightstand a beautiful apple that he had placed
out the previous evening to have with breakfast."

The modern life of Genesis began during the middle decades of the nineteenth century, as the forces of modernity came of age—science, historical scholarship, and the vast social changes wrought by the Industrial Revolution. Assumptions about how to understand the Bible, once widely shared, became fractured and fragmented. Increasingly, the old questions that Genesis had traditionally answered—about God, the cosmos, and human origins and destiny—seemed to be open-ended or even unanswerable. New ways of seeing were needed, which would bind up the fragments and provide a point from which to view things truly. The Word and the world became estranged in various ways, and we are still working on how to reconcile them.

Slavery and Emancipation

The decisive break with tradition in the United States—which had long been biblically oriented—came with the Civil War. As the historian Mark Noll emphasizes, the Civil War was, among other things, a theological crisis, in which warring interpretations of Genesis were finally adjudicated by bloody war.[1] The theological problem was the legitimacy of slavery. Three positions were generally advanced: the Bible supports slavery, the Bible opposes slavery, and slavery is wrong no matter what the Bible says. This unresolved conflict of biblical interpretation led to the devastation of the war.

The chief biblical proof-text for the pro-slavery position was the story of Noah's drunkenness in Genesis 9.[2] As Alexander Crummell, a prominent free African American, noted in 1862, "the opinion that the sufferings and the slavery of the Negro race are the consequence of the curse of Noah [is a] general, almost universal, opinion in the Christian world."[3] But, as he and other abolitionists pointed out, the biblical text does not support this interpretation. The text says (in the King James Version, which was the standard of the times):

> Noah began to be an husbandman, and he planted a vineyard: And he drank of the wine, and was drunken; and he was uncovered within his tent. And Ham, the father of Canaan, saw the nakedness of his father, and told his two brethren without. And Shem and Japheth took a garment, and laid it upon both their shoulders, and went backward, and covered the nakedness of their father; and their faces were backward, and they saw not their father's nakedness. And Noah awoke from his wine, and knew what his younger son had done unto him. And he said, Cursed be Canaan; a servant of servants shall he be unto his brethren. And he said, Blessed be Yahweh, God of Shem; and Canaan shall be his servant. God shall enlarge Japheth, and he shall dwell in the tents of Shem; and Canaan shall be his servant. (Genesis 9:20–27)

This colorful story features a flawed hero who can't hold his liquor and a strange curse on his grandson, Canaan—even though it was Canaan's father, Ham, who was at fault in seeing his father's nakedness. This is a story about shame within the patriarchal family and the patriarch's curses and blessings that shape the destiny of his descendants. The curse on Canaan provides a foreshadowing and justification of God's later decision to take away the land from the Canaanites and give it to the Israelites, who were descendants of Shem. God fulfilled Noah's curse by turning the Canaanites into slaves in Shem's tents. The curse is, in this respect, a justification for God's grant of the Promised Land to Abraham.

Since this is the first story in Genesis to mention slavery, it was often taken by later interpreters to be a justification for the institution of slavery. After the rise of the African slave trade, it was reinterpreted as a justification for the enslavement of Africans, since Ham (Canaan's father) is, according to the biblical genealogy, the ancestor of several African peoples. As the Table of Nations relates, "Ham's sons were Cush and Egypt and Put and Canaan" (Genesis 10:6). "Cush" refers to the land of Ethiopia, south of Egypt, and "Put" refers to Libya, west of Egypt. Since three out of four of Ham's sons were African, Ham came to be regarded as the ancestor of all Africans. However—and this is a crucial point—the curse is not directed against Ham or at all of his sons. It is only directed at Canaan. But

Canaan has no African descendants. The Table of Nations tells us who his children are:

> Canaan begat his firstborn, Sidon, and Heth and the Jebusites and the Amorites and the Girgashites and the Hivites and the Arkites and the Sinites and the Arvadites and the Zemarites and the Hamatites. (Genesis 10:15–18)

These are all Canaanite peoples, who lived in western Asia. The later use of this passage to justify the enslavement of Africans is simply wrong, a misreading of the plain text of Genesis.

The misinterpretation of this passage was pointed out by many abolitionists before and during the Civil War. Crummell noted these flaws in his 1862 article, appropriately titled "The Negro Race Not Under a Curse: An Examination of Genesis 9:25." This misinterpretation of Genesis, he wrote,

> is found in books written by learned men; and it is repeated in lectures, speeches, sermons, and common conversation. So strong and tenacious is the hold which it has taken upon the mind of Christendom, that it seems almost impossible to uproot it. Indeed, it is an almost foregone conclusion, that the Negro race is an accursed race, weighed down, even to the present, beneath the burden of an ancestral malediction.[4]

Crummell advanced the usual refutations. By 1862, however, the argument was being carried on not just in sermons and newspapers, but on bloody battlefields across America.

Later that year, Abraham Lincoln issued the Emancipation Proclamation, which abolished slavery in the rebellious states. In his decree he took no stand on biblical interpretation. But in his most profound comments on the Civil War—his Second Inaugural Address in 1865—he described more directly the theological crisis and his biblical justification for abolishing slavery. With great literary skill and theological acuity, he described the conflict in biblical terms, using words drawn directly from Genesis.[5] He proclaimed:

> Both [sides] read the same Bible and pray to the same God, and each invokes His aid against the other. It may seem strange that any men should dare to ask a just God's assistance in wringing their bread from the sweat of other men's faces, but let us judge not, that we be not judged.

Although the two sides in the conflict read the same Bible, they read it differently. Lincoln ignores the most contested biblical text, Noah's curse of Canaan, but refers instead to an earlier curse—God's judgment of Adam. In the King James Version, God famously says: "In the sweat of thy face shalt thou eat bread, till thou return unto the ground; for out of it wast thou taken" (Genesis 3:19). Hard toil is Adam's punishment for disobeying God's command in Eden.

Lincoln's language echoes the dignity of the Bible, as he reframes its words to make his theological point:

"It may seem strange that any men should dare to ask a just God's assistance in wringing their bread from the sweat of other men's faces." God's words to Adam in Genesis 3:19, "In the sweat of *thy* face shalt thou eat bread," are a silent rebuke to the slaveholder. Lincoln's rephrasing of Genesis convicts the pro-slavery side of impiety, since they thwart God's direct command, and of arrogance, since they "dare to ask a just God's assistance" in their unjust cause. His adroit reframing of Genesis lifts the biblical controversy over slavery to a new level, in which the Bible unequivocally condemns it as a distortion of God's plan for humanity. Men are cursed to work for their own bread. The institution of slavery—"wringing their bread from the sweat of other men's faces"—is a clear violation of God's word. It is a sin of pride and disobedience, much like Adam's original sin.

Lincoln's subtle interpretation of Genesis 3:19 contests the pro-slavery interpretation of Genesis 9:25 and other biblical passages.[6] It may be the "same Bible," but the Southern reading is "strange," since it violates the words and meaning of God's command. Yet, at the moment that he defeats the pro-slavery argument by citing Genesis, he also seeks to conciliate the two sides by reframing the words of Jesus: "let us judge not, that we be not judged." Here Lincoln turns Jesus's admonition to the angry crowd, "Judge not, lest ye be judged" (Matthew 7:1), into an admonition to both sides of the conflict, including himself. Lincoln interprets Genesis with great sensitivity to advance the justice of the abolition of slavery, but then pivots to another biblical text to advance compassion for the adversary, who is facing total defeat.

Lincoln's profound use of the Bible gave moral authority to the decisive exegesis that was occurring on the battlefield. Yet, even as he used the Bible to justify his cause and to bind up the nation's wounds, the old world of biblical interpretation was giving way. As Noll comments:

> the Civil War . . . effectively handed the business of the theologians over to the generals to decide by ordeal what the Bible meant. As things worked out, military coercion determined that, at least for the purposes of American public policy, the Bible did not support slavery. [This verdict], though never self-consciously adopted by all Americans in all circumstances, has been followed *since* the Civil War. That course is an implicit national agreement not to base public policy of any consequence on interpretations of Scripture.[7]

The theological crisis of the Civil War was also a crisis in the life of Genesis. In common with the other trends of secularization—science, scholarship, industrialization—the Word and the world grew farther apart. The public square in America became increasingly nonsectarian, as America became more hospitable to Catholics, Jews, and other immigrants who came to its shores. The recession of biblically based Protestantism as a political order opened the space for a more tolerant nation. Genesis—in its conflicting interpretations—no longer provided a viable guide for governance.

The Second Sex

The abolition movement included many prominent women, for whom the desire for emancipation had an added resonance. The same story in Genesis that Lincoln cited to condemn the institution of slavery is the chief biblical proof-text for women's servitude to men. God curses Eve with hard labor in pregnancy and patriarchal domination: "Your desire shall be to your husband, and he shall rule over you" (Genesis 3:16). The plain meaning of this divine punishment is unequivocal, and it has been an axiom in Western consciousness for millennia. Yet if the institution of slavery is wrong —an institution that exists in many biblical texts— then perhaps judgments of right and wrong should be independent of what the Bible says. This was the view of many radical abolitionists. William Lloyd Garrison argued in 1845:

> To say that everything in the Bible is to be believed, simply because it is found in that volume, is equally absurd and pernicious. . . . To discard a portion of Scripture is not necessarily to reject the truth, but may be the highest evidence that one can give of his love of truth.[8]

Spinoza's old distinction between the meaning of Scripture and the truth of things hit home in the moral debate over slavery and biblical interpretation.

In addition to the possibility of moral truths that depart from Scripture, abolitionists could also appeal to biblical texts that articulate a broader view of human equality. According to Genesis 1, all humans—both men and women—are created in God's image. As the King James Version renders it:

> God said, Let us make man in our image, after our likeness: and let them have dominion over the fish of the sea, and over the fowl of the air, and over the cattle, and over all the earth, and over every creeping thing that creepeth upon the earth. So God created man in his own image, in the image of God created he him; male and female created he them. (Genesis 1:26–27)

This text clearly expresses the principle of human equality, regardless of race or gender. Slaves, women, and free men are endowed by their Creator with equal dignity.

Among the radical abolitionists were a group of remarkable women who also formed the first wave of the women's rights movement in America. These women marshaled Genesis for both emancipatory projects. Sarah Grimké, one of the most eloquent of the radical abolitionists, appealed to Genesis 1 in her abolitionist writings and in her *Letters on the Equality of the Sexes and the Condition of Women* (1838):

We must first view woman at the period of her creation. . . . In all this sublime description of the creation of man, (which is a generic term including man and woman,) there is not one particle of difference intimated as existing between them. They were both made in the image of God; dominion was given to both over every other creature, but not over each other. Created in perfect equality, they were expected to exercise the viceregency intrusted to them by their Maker, in harmony and love.[9]

God created man and woman together, both "in the image of God." The women's movement was born in the fire of the abolition movement, and appealed to the same biblical principles of Genesis 1. After the Civil War accomplished the emancipation of slaves, abolitionist women continued to press their cause for the emancipation of women.

Another prominent abolitionist was Elizabeth Cady Stanton, who edited the first feminist biblical commentary, *The Woman's Bible*, in 1895. In this book she combined passion for women's rights with an awareness of the new wave of European biblical scholarship. She proclaims a theological revolution: "Come, come, my conservative friend, wipe the dew off your spectacles, and see that the world is moving." Since "the Scriptures . . . bear the impress of fallible man," it cannot be taken as authoritative in every part.[10] Naturally, she praises the view of women's equality in Genesis 1, which she argues was subverted by the later writer of Genesis 3:

> It is evident that some wily writer, seeing the perfect equality of man and woman in the first chapter, felt it important for the dignity and dominion of man to effect woman's subordination in some way.[11]

Stanton knew that biblical scholars had argued that Genesis 1:26–27 and Genesis 3:16 were from different sources. The subordination of women in the latter was therefore due to the eccentric imaginings of a "wily writer," and owed nothing to divine revelation. She anchors her defense of women's rights in the findings of biblical scholarship. As in the case against slavery, moral judgment appeals to a truth that is independent of Scripture, or that is perceived unevenly among the texts of Genesis. In this case, the writer of Genesis 1 perceived the truth of gender equality, which the writer of Genesis 3 sought to undermine.

Shortly after the publication of *The Woman's Bible*, the National American Woman Suffrage Association announced that it had "no official connection with the so-called 'Woman's Bible.'" It was too controversial for its time. But the argument for women's equality in the context of biblical criticism and modern science had been made. The seeds planted by Grimké, Stanton, and others were to blossom in the work of other women writers in the nineteenth and twentieth centuries.[12] One of the greatest of these—and one of the greatest modern poets—is Emily Dickinson, a contemporary of Grimké and Stanton, who wove her reimaginings of Genesis into a radical and distinctively modern perception of the world.

Uncertain Certainty

The task of the poet, according to Emily Dickinson, is to "Tell all the Truth but tell it slant."[13] The truth is too vast and unknowable to capture in words, but a great poem provides an angled glimpse of reality, so that it is seen with fresh eyes by the attentive reader. This is how Dickinson's poetry works—through her art she illuminates fragments of the inner and outer landscape of the modern world. Using traditional diction, laced with biblical allusion, she conjure bursts of vision. In her words, "The Truth must dazzle gradually / Or every man be blind."[14]

Dickinson grew up in a New England that was ruled by a stern Calvinist faith, but there were new influences in the air, spread by radical abolitionists like Garrison and Grimké, and by Transcendentalists and freethinkers like Emerson, Thoreau, and Whitman. Theodore Parker, a radical abolitionist and Unitarian minister, is a lesser known figure of the time, but was a very popular speaker in New England before the Civil War. Dickinson comments in a letter, "I heard that he was 'poison.' Then I like poison very well."[15] Parker had studied the new European biblical scholarship in seminary, and he distilled his knowledge in sermons to his fellow New Englanders. In his memoirs he recalls his seminary education in the Bible:

> I studied carefully the latest critics and interpreters, especially the German. I soon found that the Bible is a collection of quite heterogeneous books, most of them anonymous, or bearing names of doubtful authors, collected, none knows how, or when, or by whom. . . . As I found the Bible was the work of men, so I also found that the Christian Church was no more divine than the British State, a Dutchman's Shop or an Austrian's Farm. The miraculous, infallible Bible, and the miraculous, infallible Church, disappeared when they were closely looked at; and I found the Fact of History quite different from the pretension of Theology.[16]

This is the notorious "poison"—which debunks the infallibility of the Bible and the Church—that Dickinson liked so well.

For Dickinson the dialectical movement of doubt is the source of illumination—not the Bible, the Church, or the articles of doctrine. She adopted the hymnic form to praise a post-traditional sensibility, which nonetheless retains the religious capacity of transformation. She praises the "Sweet skepticism of the Heart— / That knows—and does not know—," while fashioning in her poetry flashes of transcendence, which dwell "In Genesis' new house, / Durable as dawn."[17]

Since she savored the notorious "poison" of modern ideas about the Bible, Dickinson read the book of Genesis as a collection of fictions. In the dialectic of her "sweet skepticism," she acknowledged the stories' limitations as legend, but also drew on them as a resource for her poetic imagination. Its stories are like children's tales, which one outgrows in adulthood:

> Children—matured—are wiser—mostly—
> Eden—a legend—dimly told—
> Eve and the Anguish—Grandame's story—[18]

Like Grimké and Stanton in the nascent women's movement, she sees the story of Eve's anguish (she avoids the theological freight of "sin" or "curse") as a fiction. It is merely a "Grandame's story" (perhaps also hinting that the legendary Eve is our grandmother and "grand dame"). But this maturity is ambivalent, since "Children – matured – are wiser – mostly." Not all adults gain wisdom. Her playful irony ("mostly") deflates the seriousness of her biblical reflections. Yet she also hints at unseen depths in the Eden story, which is "a legend – dimly told." The adverb "dimly" suggests an atmosphere of hidden things, a hint that the brief reference to "the Anguish" intensifies. The story may yet connect to deeper truths about reality.

Dickinson clarifies her view of the depth of the biblical stories in one of her letters, where she recalls how at the dawn of her poetic career she "fell to reading the Old & New Testament":

I had known it as an arid book but looking I saw
how infinitely wise & how merry it is. Anybody
that knows grammar must admit the surpassing
splendor & force of its speech, but the fathomless
gulfs of meaning . . . has any one fathomed that
sea?[19]

As a master of poetic language she perceives "the surpassing splendor & force of its speech," from which she
draws generously in her own speech. Her focus on its
diction and its "fathomless gulfs of meaning" brings a
modern literary sensibility to the text. The Bible is no
longer an infallible revelation, but a work of art, a book
"infinitely wise & . . . merry," which illuminates and en-
tertains—much like her own verse. She adds, "I know
those to whom those words are very near & necessary,
I wish they were more so to me." Dickinson is no longer a simple believer—she is on the other side of tradition—but she recognizes that the biblical stories are
still, as she says, "great bars of sunlight in many a shady
heart."[20]

To a skeptical heart, however, the Bible is an ancient
book, a beloved but also eccentric antique text. From
this vantage point, its faults are sometimes glaring. In a
bitingly satirical poem, she rewords the Calvinist "Articles of Doctrinal Belief" that she learned as a child,
according to which "the Scriptures of the Old and
New Testaments . . . were composed by holy men as
they were moved by the Holy Ghost."[21] In Dickinson's
revision:

> The Bible is an antique Volume—
> Written by faded Men
> At the suggestion of Holy Spectres—[22]

The doctrinal "holy men . . . moved by the Holy Ghost" are now "faded men"—anonymous and indistinct—who write "At the suggestion of Holy Spectres." The latter seems to be a group of ordinary ghosts, or perhaps more likely, a vivid imagination, which now "suggests," rather than providing plenary inspiration. Doctrinal belief about the Bible has been superseded by ironic deflation, compounded by her final line, which gives a more favorable opinion of Greek myth:

> Orpheu's Sermon captivated—
> It did not condemn.

The hardness of biblical doctrine, as taught by the Calvinist Church, is itself condemned in this line, as the biblical legacy of the "faded Men" is contrasted with the sweet poetry of Orpheus, who is "a warbling Teller." Dickinson does not restrain her critical judgment of biblical tradition, even as she elsewhere grants the "surpassing splendor" of its language and its "gulfs of meaning." Her heart's skepticism moves in both directions, between critique and imaginative appropriation.

The same movement in found in her reflections on the Garden of Eden. In the verse addressed above she describes the story as a "legend—dimly told," and she confesses in a letter, "I have never believed [Paradise] to be a superhuman site."[23] She appropriates the biblical language of Eden to indicate a human site, a condition of awareness and bliss that is always possible. As she says in the same letter, "Eden is always eligible." The formerly superhuman site is now a site in a personal landscape of spiritual transformation. As elsewhere in the motion of "sweet skepticism," the delights of Eden are laced with eroticism. In her famous poem "Wild Nights" the ecstasy of sexuality is figured as "Rowing in Eden." The superhuman has become the wholly human, with the undertone of eroticism in the Garden of Eden story transmuted into the language of passionate love.

In a deceptively simple poem, Dickinson refigures the Eden story into a parable of modern consciousness, with its losses and gains, much as the Eden story itself describes the passage from childlike innocence to mature—and conflicted—experience. This is a recasting of the biblical story into a new idiom, homely and familiar, with its truths told slant.

> Eden is that old-fashioned House
> We dwell in every day
> Without suspecting our abode
> Until we drive away.
>
> How fair on looking back, the Day
> We sauntered from the Door –
> Unconscious our returning,
> But discover it no more.[24]

The first stanza describes Eden through the metaphorical vehicle of an "old-fashioned house." This metaphor deflates the exotic, superhuman quality of Eden into a site so ordinary that, "Without suspecting our abode," we do not perceive that it is paradise. Only when we unthinkingly "drive away" (in a horse and buggy perhaps) do we realize what we have lost. Note that the repeated "we" draws the reader into a shared perception, and the present tense of the verbs make the loss a timeless and repeated experience.

The memory of Eden—of youth, innocence, and even a childlike faith in the Eden story—comes to consciousness "on looking back." The simple act of leaving the house, by foot and buggy, is now refigured as a quasi-biblical event, mapped onto the banishment of Adam and Eve from Eden. Rather than being driven out of Eden by God, past the entry guarded by fierce creatures, our exile occurred "the Day / We sauntered from the Door—." There is nothing superhuman about our expulsion from paradise; we simply walked away.

Finally—as the verbs turn back to the durative present—even as we look back in our memory, paradise is gone: "Unconscious our returning, / But discover it no more." The old-fashioned house has become gossamer, "a legend—dimly told," which once dwelled in us but is no more. The bliss of innocence is unrecoverable. We live in a more fragmented world, in which mature experience cancels out the simplicity of such innocent comforts. The old-fashioned abode has become a figment of memory, a figure of loss and desire.

Dickinson knows that the story of Eden is a legend found in "an antique Volume." But she perceives its literary capacity for truth, and she provides a poetic commentary in which Eden becomes once again "eligible" for modern times. In her commentary, she explains what Eden is, and why and how we possess it no longer. There are many truths in her modern revision of the Eden story, but as ever, she tells them slant. The movement of her heart's skepticism is ever nimble, not resting in "sere certainty." As she writes:

> Of Paradise' existence
> All we know
> Is the uncertain certainty—[25]

Parables

Dickinson's great burst of poetic composition coincided with the Civil War. The intensity of the times provoked her genius. World War I provoked another great outpouring of artistic imagination, including the most haunting of modern writers, Franz Kafka. His most famous unfinished novel (all of his novels are unfinished), *The Trial* was begun in August 1914, a few weeks after the outbreak of the Great War. Kafka was declared unfit for combat—an apt judgment for Kafka, who mockingly described himself as "unfit for this earth."[26]

Like Dickinson, Kafka drew on the Bible as an inspiration and resource for his literary imagination. He approached the Genesis stories as fictions that—when pressed far enough—may be coaxed into yielding flashes of truth. As the canine protagonist says in Kafka's late story, "Investigations of a Dog":

> it is just this greater sense of possibility that stirs us so deeply when we listen to those old and strangely simple stories. Here and there we hear a suggestive word and we would almost like to leap to our feet, if we did not feel the weight of the centuries upon us.[27]

For Kafka, who was fascinated with his half-forgotten Jewish traditions, the stories of Genesis were gems to be savored in order to glimpse that "greater sense of possibility," which often pervades his own stories. As Walter Benjamin observed, the intensity of Kafka's fictions seems to "metamorphosize life into Scripture."[28] He does this, in part, by weaving fragments and allusions to Genesis into his texts.

The Trial, is usually—and rightly—compared with the biblical book of Job. As Max Brod commented, Josef K's final complaints—"Where was the judge he'd never seen? Where was the high court he'd never reached?"—are echoes of Job's laments, and the whole book resonates with "the old problem of Job."[29] Primo Levi beautifully articulates this dimension of Kafka's novel: "So this is it, this is human destiny: we can be persecuted and punished for a crime which has not even been committed, which is obscure and which will never be revealed to us by the 'court.'"[30] This intensification of Job's predicament is obvious enough, yet, as is often the case, the density of Kafka's prose defeats a simple reading of Josef K. as a modern Job. A countervailing set of allusions, to the Garden of Eden story, complicates the story and makes Josef K.'s trial a much more ambiguous predicament.

The novel begins with a curious line: "Someone must have slandered Josef K., for one morning, without having done anything wrong, he was arrested." Like Job, Josef K. seems to be an innocent man, since he has not "done anything wrong." But the word translated as "wrong," *Böse* in German, also has a stronger meaning, "evil." As Breon Mitchell observes about the difficulty of translating this line, this word, "when applied to the actions of an adult, reverberates with moral and philosophical overtones ranging from the story of the Fall in the Garden of Eden to Nietzsche's discussion of the origins of morality in *Jenseits von Gut und Böse (Beyond Good and Evil)*."[31] Job, we are told at the outset of the biblical book, is a totally innocent and righteous man (Job 1:1). Yet Josef K., who has done nothing evil, may not be entirely innocent.

The shadow of the Eden story—with its themes of knowledge, transgression, shame, and guilt—becomes clearer in the opening scene, when the guards appear in his boarding house to arrest him. The guards steal K's breakfast, although they offer—for a price—to buy him another. K. retreats to his bedroom:

He threw himself onto his bed and took from the nightstand a beautiful apple that he had placed out the previous evening to have with breakfast. Now it was his entire breakfast, and in any case, as he verified with the first large bite, a much better breakfast than he could have had from the filthy all-night café through the grace of his guards. He felt confident and at ease.[32]

This strange scene recalls—with a comical touch—the transgression in Eden. In European tradition, the fruit of the Tree of the Knowledge of Good and Evil had long been identified as an apple, based on the Latin homonym of "evil" and "apple." Here K. eats "a beautiful apple" ("einen schönen Apfel") and "with the first large bite . . . felt confident and at ease." This is a curious deflation of Original Sin, since K. is really just sneaking a breakfast in place of the one that the guards have stolen. Yet, suddenly, he considers committing suicide— which refashions God's warning, "On the day you eat of it you shall surely die" (Genesis 2:17). K. dismisses this thought as irrational, and instead downs two shots of schnapps. This scene illustrates what Roberto Calasso calls the "amalgam of the outrageously comic and the appalling—a gift of Kafka's."[33]

A deeper resonance of this scene is signaled by the allusion to the Eden story. As Ritchie Robertson comments, "K. may be morally ignorant at the very beginning of the novel, but the first effect of his arrest is to arouse in him the knowledge of good and evil, symbolized by his eating 'einen schönen Apfel.'"[34] K. now knows of his presumptive guilt. As one of the guards explains, "the Law . . . is attracted by guilt."[35] Although K. protests his innocence, he now knows something of his guilt, even if it is a rumor or accusation. Then he eats the apple, the symbol of the Knowledge of Good and Evil, which gives him a momentary feeling of confidence and ease, before he feels intense self-loathing.

This scene compounds biblical allusion with theological irony. K. briefly refers to "the grace of the guards," who offered to buy him breakfast "from the filthy all-night café." The language of "grace" ("Gnade") seems out of place, yet heightens the biblical and theological tenor of the scene. The lowly guards, however, are in no position to provide grace. K. has eaten the apple, but the Knowledge of Good and Evil seems to consist only of knowledge that he has been arrested, accompanied by a vague self-consciousness of guilt.

After his dressing gown is deemed unsuitable, K. dons his best black suit (perhaps an ironic counterpart to Adam and Eve dressing to hide their nakedness after eating the forbidden fruit) and he faces the inspector for his first interrogation. The interrogation incongruously occurs in Fräulein Burstner's bedroom, providing an erotic backdrop to the accusation. However, unlike the interrogation by God in the Garden of Eden, the inspector's interrogation is not very imposing. He informs K.:

These gentlemen and I are merely marginal figures in your affair, and in fact know almost nothing about it . . . I can't report that you've been accused of anything, or more accurately, I don't know if you have. You've been arrested, that's true, but that's all I know.[36]

Not only is lack of knowledge the norm, but the accusation doesn't even change the form of K.'s life. The inspector continues, "You're under arrest, certainly, but that's not meant to keep you from carrying on your profession. Nor are you to be hindered in the course of your ordinary life."

K.'s life does not change outwardly, but his self-consciousness has irrevocably changed, now that he has gained his ambiguous knowledge. He becomes increasingly obsessed with his trial, until at the end he calmly waits for his executioners, dressed once again in his best black suit. Even at the end, K.'s guilt or innocence remains ambiguous. However, in his diary Kafka confesses that Josef K. is indeed "the guilty one," who at the end is "executed . . . with a gentler hand, more pushed aside than struck down."[37] He has eaten from the apple, but he does not know what he is guilty of, nor why the Law has been drawn to him.

Part of the problem is that K. is not a self-reflective person. As he admits to himself, "he generally didn't make it a practice to learn from experience." Yet he seems to have gained some awareness of the possibility of guilt. As he says to Fräulein Burstner that first night, "it may have been that the commission of inquiry realized I'm guiltless or at least not quite as guilty as they thought."[38]

The allusion to the Garden of Eden story makes Josef K. a modern Adam who is confronted with a mysterious guilt. Yet the comic quality of the opening scene makes the overlay of Adam onto Josef K. a partial and ironic one. K. is a pompous banker and a moral mediocrity. The guards are corrupt fools. The inspector is ignorant. Throughout the novel, the depictions of the legal proceedings are laced with comic details. As Brod relates:

> When Kafka read aloud himself, this humor became particularly clear. Thus, for example, we friends of his laughed quite immoderately when he first let us hear the first chapter of *The Trial*. And he himself laughed so much that there were moments when he couldn't read any further.[39]

The scene where K. eats the "beautiful apple" is comical in its details—unlike the Garden of Eden story—yet at the same time it is a dark vision of helplessness in a world of impersonal surveillance and punishment. (Compare the scene in the *Metamorphosis* where Gregor's father assaults his bizarrely transformed son by throwing apples at him, leaving him lethally wounded.) The intensity of the depiction and the background of biblical resonance make the story into a radical transformation of Genesis—and Job. It is a peculiarly Kafkaesque Scripture—in turns dreamlike, harrowing, comical, and profound. Its stylistic and spiritual force, in a landscape without God, echoes ironically the laconic depth of the biblical stories.

Kafka returned to the stories of Genesis in a series of aphorisms composed in 1917–18, at the height of the Great War.[40] This text represent Kafka's most spiritual period, as he healed from his first attack of tuberculosis and contemplated the destruction of civilization around him. In the aphorisms he returns to some of the riddles of Josef K.—How do we address our condition of guilt and ignorance? Is moral self-awareness possible? In his reflections, Kafka turns the stories of Genesis into parables that offer momentary consolations to the modern world.

Robert Alter aptly describes Kafka's use of Genesis in his parables: "Kafka's imagination is compelled by the structure of the biblical text and he walks around it, trying to find some odd back-entrance into it for himself."[41] So, for example, he finds an odd entry—and a conceivable but impossible ending—for the Tower of Babel story:

> If it had been possible to build the Tower of Babel
> without ascending it, it would have been
> permitted.[42]

This thought experiment is paradoxical, for how could someone build a tower without ascending it? The very suggestion seems pointless and self-defeating. Yet there is a serious implication, for the Tower—which ascends up to heaven—is prohibited in Genesis precisely because by ascending it the people of Babel would transcend the human world. Yahweh says to himself, "This is what they have begun to do. Now there will be no restraining them from whatever they plan to do" (Genesis 11:6). God destroys the Tower of Babel to thwart their unstoppable ambitions—their all-too-human hubris.

But, Kafka muses, if we could build without ascending, it would be allowed. We could transcend the ordinary world only if we resist the temptation to climb the Tower to heaven. But he states this as an unreal condition: "If it had been possible." Since it is impossible, we are fated to remain here in our ordinary world, scattered, confused, and weak. The ideal is thinkable by means of the parable, but reality restrains us. Kafka finds a peculiar back way into the myth of the Tower of Babel and turns it—quite brilliantly—into a paradox about the limits of transcendence.

Kafka unpacks the sense of his parable in a letter:

> In theory, there exists a perfect earthly possibility for happiness, that is, to believe in the decisively divine and *not* to aspire to attain it. This possibility for happiness is as blasphemous as it is unattainable.[43]

In the parable he imagines the people building the Tower without ascending it. In the letter's more abstract formulation, one believes in the "decisively divine" without aspiring to it. This is the "perfect earthly possibility for happiness." But it remains a possibility, thinkable but not achievable. Since it is "as blasphemous as it is unattainable," it returns us, on a different level, to the Tower of Babel, which is the emblem of the blasphemous and unattainable. Through the layered paradoxes, we glimpse a vision of what earthly happiness would be, even if it is not available in reality. This is the "greater sense of possibility" that Kafka sees in the Genesis stories and that he tries to articulate for modern times.

In a similar vein, Kafka offers a conceivable alternative ending for the Garden of Eden story:

> We were created to live in paradise, and paradise was designed to serve us. Our destiny has been changed; that this has also happened with the destiny of paradise is not stated.[44]

Since paradise was made for humans, and the biblical story does not alter this purpose, paradise is presumably still available for us. While humans no longer live in paradise because of the ancient transgression and expulsion, in theory it still exists with this purpose. However, in reality our access is blocked—we don't know where paradise is, and according to Genesis it is guarded by fierce creatures—cherubim and a flaming sword (Genesis 3:24). Therefore we can glimpse this possibility only in fiction. We are poised between the reality of exile and the possibility of redemption, but the latter is unattainable. The impasse between the possible and the actual is final. And yet, as Kafka senses, the unclear destiny of paradise opens a hint of other endings. This is a real implication of the Genesis story,[45] which Kafka distills into a haunting paradox.

In other Genesis aphorisms, Kafka turns this impasse into even more complicated reflections on the human condition. Although it seems that we have been expelled from paradise, he poses the conjecture that in some sense we may never have left. This becomes a paradox of consciousness, in which, if only we could see rightly, our exile would be an illusion, and we could perceive that the world and paradise are the same, but seen from different perspectives. This is a Kafkaesque revision of Platonism, but in a monistic (not dualistic) reality:

> The expulsion from paradise is in its main aspect eternal: Thus it is true that the expulsion from paradise is final, and life in the world is unavoidable, but the eternal nature of the event makes it nevertheless possible that not only could we remain continually in paradise, but that in fact we are continually there, no matter whether we know it here or not.[46]

Like the other reflections on Genesis, this is a possible but uncertain interpretation of reality. We may remain continually in paradise, even if we do not know it. It is "possible" that we are there in actual fact. But can this possibility be brought fully to consciousness, so that we can examine whether it is a fact? This is a conjecture on Genesis, a fiction predicated on fiction, yet Kafka offers it as a possible glimmer of truth.

Like Josef K., we are burdened with deceptions and self-justifications that make us insensible to the realities of our condition. What if we were to cast off these self-deceptions? Would we see that we are already in paradise? Or would we be destroyed by the very attempt? Kafka cites another story in Genesis, when Lot's wife looks behind her to glimpse the destruction of Sodom, to illustrate this danger:

> Can you then know anything else but deception? If ever the deception is destroyed you must never look back, or you will turn into a pillar of salt.[47]

Like Lot's wife, who dared to look back, we would be destroyed without our illusions. We cannot see the truth whole. Yet the alternative is bleak—to embrace our deceptions, like Joseph K., and live a hollow life.

In a dense reflection on the Garden of Eden story, Kafka draws some of these paradoxical threads together. This reflection, as commentators have noted, may also illuminate the predicament of Josef K.:

> Since the Fall we have been essentially equal in our capacity for the Knowledge of Good and Evil. . . . No one can be content with the knowledge alone, but must strive to act in accordance with it. But the strength to do so is not given to him, hence he must destroy himself. . . . [Yet] nothing else remains for him but this final attempt. . . . Now this is an attempt he is afraid to make; he would rather annul the Knowledge of Good and Evil (the term,

"the Fall," has its origin in this fear); but what has once happened cannot be annulled, it can only be blurred. It is for this purpose that the justifications arise. The whole world is full of them; indeed the whole visible world is perhaps nothing other than the self-justification of a man who wants to find a moment of peace. An attempt to distort the fact that knowledge is already given, to make knowledge a goal still to be reached.[48]

In Kafka's complicated reflection, the knowledge of good and evil puts us in an impossible dilemma. Our innate capacity for this knowledge is not equaled by our capacity to live by it. Since we do not have the strength to live in accord with our knowledge, we adopt self-justifications and deceptions to distract us and to hide this knowledge from our self-consciousness. We try to efface this knowledge, so that we do not destroy ourselves. But in so doing, we make our lives false, like Josef K. The choices are self-destruction by living in accord with the Knowledge of Good and Evil, which we lack the strength to do, or self-delusion by filling our world with false justifications.

There is no easy solution or equilibrium within this dilemma. We either act in accord with the truth and destroy ourselves, or dull our senses with deceptions. We either turn to salt, like Lot's wife, or fill our lives with excuses. A bitter choice. Yet the parable itself shows us that at least we have the freedom to choose. This is some consolation. If we can glimpse a greater possibility, then perhaps something is gained, if only a new perspective or awareness of our failure.

As another of Kafka's parables concludes:

> One said: "Why do you resist? If you followed the parables, then you would become parables yourselves, and thus free of your daily cares."
>
> Another said: "I bet that is also a parable."
>
> The first said: "You have won."
>
> The second said: "But unfortunately only in parable."
>
> The first said: "No, in reality; in parable you have lost."[49]

Although this sequence seems dizzying or impossible, it elucidates the nature of Kafka's aphorisms and parables on Genesis. The possible is achievable only in parable. The greater sense of possibility resides in the genre of fiction.[50] But in reality, a parable is just a parable. The second speaker wins in reality by identifying the parable as a parable. But since this identification falsifies the truth that is interior to the parable, his win is a loss. He identifies the parable as fiction, but this true identification makes him lose the possibility of becoming "free of your daily cares," which exists only in parable. The dizzying motion of these entwined dualities— between the possible and the actual, knowledge and delusion, freedom and guilt—is basic to Kafka's aphorisms on Genesis.

Like Dickinson, Kafka viewed the stories of Genesis as legends that never happened, but that expose greater possibilities. The stories are at the same time impossible, redemptive, and obscure. In his imaginative revisions of Genesis, particularly in *The Trial* and the aphorisms, Kafka seeks a glimpse of truth—and even transcendence—in the midst of ordinary life, a way to lift the blinkers that we habitually wear in our daily toil. There is little certainty in these stories and conjectures, and there are always other conjectures to refute them. But occasionally they produce a radiance that we may not otherwise have seen.

Return to Realism

Nine years after Kafka's death, modern history took a dark, Kafkaesque turn—Hitler became chancellor in Germany and the Nazi era began. Later that year (1933) a massive book-burning campaign was organized at German universities. Kafka's books were cast into the flames, along with books by other Jews and "degenerates," including Einstein, Darwin, Ernest Hemingway, and Helen Keller. Western civilization was under threat. Shortly thereafter, the Nazi regime began to "cleanse" German universities of Jewish professors. One of these was Erich Auerbach, a professor of European literature. Like many other academic exiles, Auerbach found refuge at Istanbul State University in Turkey. During the war years, in the solitude of exile, he wrote his classic book, *Mimesis: The Representation of Reality in Western Literature*. This book is a brilliant tour of the conceptual styles of Western literature. Auerbach begins his story with the roots of Western literature: Homer and Genesis.

Auerbach sought to explore the multifaceted ways that Western literature represents reality, the ways that it deals with the complexities of lived existence. The negative foil for his exploration, which he never explicitly stated, was the anti-humanistic ideology of Nazism, which represented reality as a crude struggle between the German spirit and the degenerate non-Aryan races. Auerbach points to this horrific backdrop at the end of the book, where he expresses his hope:

> I hope that my study will reach its readers—both my friends of former years, if they are still alive, as well as all the others for whom it was intended. And may it contribute to bringing together again those whose love for our western history has serenely persevered.[51]

His study is an expression of love for the humane values of Western civilization, which fascism was attempting to destroy. By exploring the history of the representations of reality from Genesis to the present day, Auerbach sought to preserve the achievement of these works and their insights into the human condition. This was his war effort—a campaign for hearts and minds waged at his writing desk in Istanbul.[52]

His decision to begin his literary study with Genesis was brilliant and audacious. He embraces the fictional nature of Genesis, not as part of a controversy between religion and science, but as the starting point of Western literature. This is a perspective on Genesis that began with Herder and other romantics, but Auerbach takes it to a new level. Under Auerbach's searching eyes, Genesis is shown to be a sophisticated text with a fully developed style. Moreover, its manner of representing reality and the human condition as multilayered, problematic, and "fraught with background" provides Western literature with a major impetus for exploring reality complexly. As Robert Alter explains:

> In the famous comparison of the Odyssey with Genesis that takes up the first chapter, it is the Bible, not Homer, that emerges as the great forerunner of the representation of human life with existential seriousness in Western literature. . . . [T]he ancient Hebrew writers' engagement with what Auerbach refers to as the problematic character of everyday life and the distinctive tenor of individual experience lays the ground more than any Greek counterpart for what is announced in the book's subtitle: the representation of reality in Western literature.[53]

This argument—which is persuasive in all its essentials—places Genesis in a new light. Genesis is now a work of sophisticated literary art, whether or not one regards it as religiously authoritative. It is a classic contribution to Western literature and civilization.

Auerbach reinserts Genesis into the genealogy of Western thought as an indissoluble part of our cultural heritage and a root of the modern perception of reality. He shows that the writers of Genesis were the first to fully represent "the phenomena of historical becoming and ... the 'multilayeredness' of the human problem," and as a consequence they exercised a "determining influence upon the representation of reality in European literature."[54] These are large claims, but they are substantiated by Auerbach's meticulous reading of Genesis. The biblical writers—whom Auerbach pointedly identifies as Jewish, as an implicit rebuke to Nazi ideology—"are able to express the simultaneous existence of various layers of consciousness and the conflict between them."[55] He is talking about the writers of Genesis, but in his use of the present tense one may detect his affirmation of the rich historical consciousness of modern literature. That is, the best of modern literature derives its style of representation, in some respects, from Genesis.

The heart of Auerbach's discussion is a close reading of Genesis 22, the story where God commands Abraham to sacrifice his son Isaac. Auerbach's brilliant discussion of this short text shows not only how the biblical text represents reality in a distinctive manner, but also how to read Genesis as a complex literary work. This had never been accomplished before at such a high level. While many—including Spinoza, Dickinson, and Kafka—had come to regard Genesis as fiction, no one had brought such a detailed understanding of how literature works to the task of reading Genesis. In this respect Auerbach's scholarly achievement complements the literary achievements of Dickinson, Kafka, and others—they drew upon Genesis as a rich resource for their literature, whereas Auerbach uses his literary sensibility as a resource for reading Genesis. The modern life of Genesis derives strength from both sides—as an inspiration for literary and moral imagination and as a literary text itself.

Genesis 22 begins in a manner that is abrupt, obscure, and suggestive:

> And it came to pass after these things, that God tested Abraham. And He said to him, "Abraham!" and he said, "Here am I."

Auerbach raises some pointed questions, which the story does not answer:

> Where are the two speakers? We are not told. . . . Whence does [God] come, whence does he call to Abraham? We are not told. . . . Nor are we told anything of his reasons for [testing] Abraham so terribly. . . . [U]nexpected and mysterious, he enters the scene from some unknown height or depth.[56]

Not only is God's whereabouts unknown, but so is Abraham's:

Where he is actually, whether in Beersheba or else-where, whether indoors or in the open air, is not stated; it does not interest the narrator, the reader is not informed; and what Abraham was doing when God called to him is left in the same obscurity.[57]

In the style of this narrative—which belongs to the E source—most things are left unexpressed, hidden in the background, while a few details are illuminated in the foreground. We have no access to the thoughts and motivations of the characters, except by the hints in the terse words of the dialogue—"Abraham!" and "Here am I." God is the one who calls—seemingly from no-where—and Abraham is the one who obeys. Although this exchange seems fairly innocuous, a mere greeting or summons, if we pay close attention to the words we can sense that they already anticipate the themes of the story. God's call and Abraham's obedience—these have occurred previously in Genesis, and they activate the memories of the characters as well as of the readers. The complexities of history and memory—both God's and Abraham's—are intimated already in the initial exchange.

Abraham's journey proceeds with minimal descrip-tion, one action after another, with a brief notice of time and place:

And Abraham rose in the morning, and he saddled his ass, and he took two of his servants with him, and Isaac, his son. And he split the wood for the

sacrifice, and he rose and went to the place that
God had told him. On the third day Abraham
lifted his eyes, and he saw the place from afar.
(Genesis 22:3–4)

Auerbach comments on the spare narration of this
journey:

> That gesture [lifting up his eyes] is the only gesture,
> is indeed the only occurrence during the whole
> journey, of which we are told; and though its moti-
> vation lies in the fact that the place is elevated, its
> uniqueness still heightens the impression that the
> journey took place through a vacuum; it is as if,
> while he traveled on, Abraham had looked neither
> to the right nor to the left, had suppressed any sign
> of life in his followers and himself save only their
> footfalls.[58]

The narrative leaves out any expression of interiority—
no stress, thought, or emotion—yet at the same time
this very absence creates a tension, a building suspense.
Abraham knows that Isaac is the child of the promise,
through whom Abraham's descendants will be a great
nation and the other peoples of the world will be
blessed. Yet he must kill him, because of God's command. The unspoken tension is nearly unbearable.

The only extraneous word in this sequence is *beno*,
"his son." We already know that Isaac is his son. Moreover, the word "your son" was already attached to Isaac
in the first verse. This expression of relationship echoes

throughout the story, and points to the psychological tension in Abraham even as he remains silent. As Auerbach comments, "his silent obedience is multilayered, has background."[59] His silence hints at the complexity of a human consciousness as it strains to reconcile its clashing allegiances of obedience, hope, and love (we are explicitly told that Isaac is Abraham's beloved son in the first verse). Perhaps silence is the only plausible way to represent the intensity of this inner conflict.

These tensions come into the foreground when father and son have their one brief dialogue:

> And the two of them went on together. And Isaac spoke to Abraham, his father, saying, "My father!" And he said, "Here am I, my son." And he said, "Here is the fire and the wood, but where is the lamb for the sacrifice?" And Abraham said, "God will see to the lamb for the sacrifice, my son." And the two of them went on together. (Genesis 22:6–8)

Note the repeated key words, "father" and "son," in this tense exchange, highlighting their bond that is now at risk. The dialogue is framed by the statement "And the two of them went on together." The repetition intensifies the resonance of the words *šenehem* ("two of them") and *yaḥdav* ("together"), since it is now clear that the two will be reduced to one, and the father-son duo will not go on together. These stylistic techniques create palpable psychological depth and tension.

Auerbach comments, "their speech does not serve ... to manifest, to externalize thoughts—on the contrary, it serves to indicate thoughts which remain unexpressed."[60] One of the ways that this scene indicates unexpressed thoughts is by allusion to the earlier exchange between God and Abraham. Isaac's call to his father, "My father!" (*'avi*), recalls God's call, "Abraham! (*'av-raham*), at the story's beginning. The resemblance of these two calls is affirmed when Abraham replies, for the second time, *hinneni* ("Here am I")— the same reply to a different interlocutor. What God had commanded, Isaac now subtly questions—"where is the lamb for the sacrifice?" This is an impossible question for Abraham to answer. His reply is an evasion, a delicate lie: "God will see to the lamb for the sacrifice," adding ominously, "my son." Abraham evades the truth in order to spare Isaac the words that he dare not say.

However, Abraham's reply is retrospectively true. This adds a layer of irony onto Abraham's apparent evasion. God will indeed see to the lamb for the sacrifice—with the variation that the lamb will be a ram, which Abraham sees in the bushes when he lifts his eyes once more (verse 13; the Hebrew word *seh* In verse 7 usually means "lamb," but it can refer to caprids in general). At the moment of his reply to Isaac, Abraham seems to be lying, but in his previously mentioned capacity as a prophet (see Genesis 20:7), he seems to foretell the future, even if inadvertently. By sparing

Isaac the truth, he ends up speaking the truth all the same. The multilayered quality of this terse exchange, when we read it closely, indicates the complexities of the characters' self-consciousness, the pathos and ironies of their spoken words, and the ambiguous intricacies of God's plan.

The literary style of the Genesis writer artfully represents reality as multilayered, suggestive, and problematic. As Auerbach demonstrates, this is a profoundly new style, which has long since served as a model and guide in the literary representation of reality in Western culture:

> certain parts brought into high relief, others left obscure, abruptness, suggestive influence of the unexpressed, "background" quality, multiplicity of meanings and the need for interpretation, universal-historical claims, development of the concept of the historically becoming, and preoccupation with the problematic.[61]

Auerbach contrasts this style with that of the *Odyssey*, which has a more static technique: "all events in the foreground, displaying unmistakable meanings, few elements of historical development and of psychological perspective."[62] His description of the representational style of Genesis pertains particularly to the J and E texts. (The P texts have a different set of representational features, but are mostly not narrative texts.) Auerbach elsewhere calls this style "existential realism." With minimal details and maximal resonance, the Genesis writers created a view of reality and of human consciousness that stands as a source of Western civilization.

Auerbach's method of reading Genesis as a fully realized work of literary art does justice to the text and to its legacy. By approaching Genesis as a literary text—even if it has long also served as a source of doctrine and religious authority—he is able to discern its own sophisticated manner of representing the real. In doing so, Auerbach gives us the tools to read Genesis in a modern way—not by recourse to theological assumptions, but on the basis of careful attention to its distinctive literary artistry. Genesis itself becomes a real, palpable narrative text under Auerbach's attentive reading.

At the same time that Auerbach articulates the style of Genesis and its multilayered representation of reality, he also points to the complexity of our modern consciousness of history. In his precarious condition of exile, with Western civilization on the verge of destruction, he focused on the representation of the world in all of its complexity and contradictions, in its concrete lived problems, and at the beginning of the road he found Genesis. We see a return to realism in his precise reading of Genesis as a book, and in his powerful description of how Genesis perceives and represents reality. Genesis is now fully emancipated from its figural sense. It is now a book written by real people, which we can read not only as Jews or Christians but as participants in Western civilization. This is a return to realism in modern times, a perception of reality that the writers of Genesis staked out long ago.

But there is a further twist in this return to realism. At the same time that we can read Genesis for its literary depth and power, and for its astonishing representations of reality, this realism tends to lead us away from Genesis's own religious horizons. As Auerbach observes:

> The Scripture stories do not, like Homer's, court our favor, they do not flatter us that they may please us and enchant us—they seek to subject us, and if we refuse to be subjected we are rebels.[63]

This is the other side of modern realism. If we read the stories of Genesis as fictions—as science and scholarship have demonstrated that we must—then we are outside of the believing audience that Genesis seeks to instruct. Its realism becomes, for us, a magical realism. Since we refuse to be subjected to the authority of Genesis, we are rebels.

This is another feature of the multilayered reality of modern times. Like Auerbach in Istanbul, who in his exile could draw upon all of Western history and literature, we moderns (which in my view includes religious conservatives) can read Genesis in its real complexity only because we stand outside of the antique, medieval, and early modern worldviews that it engendered. We are rebels in that we stand outside of this historical circle. In Auerbach's words:

when, through too great a change in environment and through the awakening of a critical consciousness, this [figural framework of reality] becomes impossible, the Biblical claim to absolute authority is jeopardized; the method of interpretation is scorned and rejected, the Biblical stories become ancient legends.[64]

This is a description of modern times. We live on the far side of tradition, and the stories of Genesis have become legends. Yet, the advantage of exile is that we can read these legends with new eyes, unencumbered by the burden of ecclesiastical authority. In our exile, we can read Genesis as it is now—an astonishing book of marvelous realism and the root from which we came.

Stories of Our Alley

"This is the story of our alley—its stories, rather." So begins Naguib Mahfouz's 1959 novel *Children of the Alley*. In it Mahfouz retells the stories of Adam and Eve, Cain and Abel, Moses, Jesus, and Muhammad in a realistic manner, as if they were characters inhabiting a run-down quarter of Cairo. Not surprisingly, the Egyptian religious authorities accused Mahfouz of blasphemy, and his novel was banned. In 1994 two fundamentalist thugs, fulfilling a *fatwa* against the novel by an extremist cleric, stabbed him in the neck outside of his home. Although Mahfouz had been awarded the 1988 Nobel Prize in Literature, it was only after his death in 2006 that the book was published in his home country.[1] As the reception of this novel shows, the stories of Genesis are still involved in tangled affairs of religious orthodoxy and retribution, as they were in the days of Galileo, Spinoza, Rabelais, and other heretics.

In Mahfouz's novel, the master of the quarter is the fearsome and nearly ageless patriarch, Gebelawi, whose youngest son is Adham. One day Adham's brother Idris (whose name is a play on Iblis, Satan in the Qur'an) entices Adham to read his father's secret last will and testament. Impelled by curiosity and by his wife's desire to gain knowledge of the future, Adham breaks into his father's office and discovers the book:

> Against the right wall was an elegant table with the huge book on it, chained to the wall. Adham's throat was dry and he swallowed painfully, as if his tonsils were inflamed. He grit his teeth as if to squeeze the fear out of his quaking limbs. With the candle in his hand, he approached the table and studied the volume's cover, ornamented with gold-leafed script, then put his hand out and opened it. Only with difficulty could he control himself and concentrate his mind. He read, in slanted Persian-style script, the formula "In the name of God."[2]

Adham reads no further. His angry father discovers him in the act and banishes Adham and his wife from the mansion. Thereafter, Gebelawi becomes a recluse, and the affairs of the alley fall into the hands of corrupt overseers and thugs, making life miserable for all its inhabitants.

Conditions in the alley improve temporarily during the lives of Gabal (Moses), Rifaa (Jesus), and Qassem (Muhammad), but after brief periods of hopefulness, life reverts to normal in the alley. Corrupt gangsters resume their rule, as they have done ever since the exile of Adham. Eventually the reclusive master Gebelawi dies—representing the death of God, or of a particular conception of God. There is hope that another hidden book—a book of science—may hold the secret to better days ahead. But at the end, the corrupt and powerful overseer still rules the alley. The old stories about the patriarchs, prophets, and saviors are of no avail. As one character wearily asks, "When will our alley stop telling its tales? . . . What good have the tales done for you, poor alley?"[3]

These questions go to the heart of our narrative of the life of Genesis. We have learned to read the stories as fictions, and the ways that our alley (that is, Western civilization) has interpreted the stories are mostly fictional too. Of what use are legends whose interpretations are themselves legendary? Fictions wrapped in other fictions? Mahfouz's novel gently criticizes these self-deceptions. He once said, "I am criticizing the legend through reality."[4] The claim of the real makes us see the legends as legends, as mere stories of the alley.

A small word may point us in another direction, offering a more positive answer to these questions. Why do we still tell these tales? Because they are stories of "our" alley, not of someone else's or no one's. This is the place where our ancestors lived, and it is where we still live, breathe, rejoice, and struggle. We are the "children of our alley" (*awlād ḥāratinā*, the Arabic title of Mahfouz's book). These are our stories, whether we accept them or rebel against them. It is likely that our alley will never stop telling its tales, since they are part of our inheritance, woven into the shared memory of who we are. Many people don't read Genesis anymore—which

I think is a loss—but we still fight over the meanings and consequences of the stories, and over their myriad interpretations in Western culture. The book may seem to be difficult or indecipherable, as if it were "ornamented with gold-leafed script . . . in slanted Persian-style." It may be fearsome, even blasphemous, to read it in a modern style, as a compendium of our alley's legends. But it is unavoidable, since they are our stories, and we are their children.

ca. 10th–6th centuries BCE	The Book of Genesis
6th century BCE	The Book of Ezekiel
3rd century BCE	The Septuagint
3rd–1st century BCE	The Book of Enoch
2nd century BCE	Jubilees
2nd century BCE–1st century CE	Dead Sea Scrolls
1st century CE	Philo of Alexandria, *Allegorical Interpretation*
1st century	The New Testament
2nd century	*The Secret Revelation of John*
4th century	The Desert Fathers
4th century	*Genesis Rabbah*
ca. 415	Augustine, *The Literal Meaning of Genesis*
ca. 1075	Rashi, *Commentary on Genesis*

INTRODUCTION: The Life of Genesis

1. Walter Benjamin, "The Task of the Translator," in *Illuminations: Essays and Reflections,* ed. Hannah Arendt (New York: Schocken Books, 1968), 73.

2. Erich Auerbach, *Mimesis: The Representation of Reality in Western Literature* (Princeton: Princeton University Press, 1953), 15.

3. Friedrich Nietzsche, *On the Advantage and Disadvantage of History for Life* (Indianapolis: Hackett Publishing, 1980), 38.

4. Frank Kermode, "The Uses of Error," *The Uses of Error and Other Essays* (Cambridge, MA: Harvard University Press, 1991), 4.

5. Auerbach, *Mimesis,* 310. Auerbach is primarily concerned with apocalyptic figuralism, in which events contain a prophecy of their future fulfillment. I include Platonic figuralism, granting, of course, that the different kinds of figuralism have distinctive traits. Auerbach perhaps understates the importance of Platonic figuralism because of his interest in nascent historical consciousness (see *Mimesis,* 196). My terms, Platonic and apocalyptic, correspond to the traditional rhetorical terms, allegory and typology, and serve to emphasize their philosophical orientation.

CHAPTER 1: The Genesis of Genesis

1. For more details, see Ronald Hendel, "Historical Context," in *The Book of Genesis: Composition, Reception, and Interpretation*, eds. Craig A. Evans, Joel N. Lohr, and David L. Petersen (Leiden: Brill, 2012), 51–81; and Angel Sáenz-Badillos, *A History of the Hebrew Language* (Cambridge: Cambridge University Press, 1993), 56–62.

2. See further Richard E. Friedman, *Who Wrote the Bible?* (New York: Simon & Schuster, 1987); Robert S. Kawashima, "Sources and Redaction," in *Reading Genesis: Ten Methods*, ed. Ronald Hendel (New York: Cambridge University Press, 2010), 47–70; and Joel S. Baden, *The Composition of the Pentateuch* (New Haven: Yale University Press, 2012).

3. This word is obscure, possibly "drummers" (from the root *mḥṣ*, "striker") or "pipers" (from the root *ḥṣr*, "reed pipe").

4. Trans. Andrew R. George, *The Babylonian Gilgamesh Epic* (2 vols.; Oxford: Oxford University Press, 2003), 713; see also George, *The Epic of Gilgamesh* (London: Penguin, 2003).

5. See further Tryggve N. D. Mettinger, *The Eden Narrative: A Literary and Religio-historical Study of Genesis 2–3* (Winona Lake, IN: Eisenbrauns, 2007).

6. Trans. Benjamin R. Foster, *Before the Muses: An Anthology of Akkadian Literature* (3rd ed., Bethesda, MD: CDL Press, 2005), 488–89.

7. See Richard J. Clifford, *Creation Accounts in the Ancient Near East and in the Bible* (Washington, DC: Catholic Biblical Association, 1994).

8. See Mark S. Smith, *The Priestly Vision of Genesis 1* (Minneapolis: Fortress Press, 2010).

9. Hendel, "Historical Context."

10. Cf. Alan Dundes's definition of myth as "a sacred nar-

rative explaining how the world or humans came to be in their present form," in *The Flood Myth*, ed. Dundes (Berkeley: University of California Press, 1988), 1. On the genres of Genesis, see further Ronald Hendel, *Remembering Abraham: Culture, Memory, and History in the Hebrew Bible* (New York: Oxford University Press, 2005), 98–107.

CHAPTER 2: The Rise of the Figural Sense

1. See James L. Kugel and Rowan A. Greer, *Early Biblical Interpretation* (Philadelphia: Westminster Press, 1986); Michael Fishbane, *Biblical Interpretation in Ancient Israel* (Oxford: Clarendon Press, 1985).

2. James L. Kugel, *The Bible As It Was* (Cambridge, MA: Harvard University Press, 1997); see also his expanded version, *Traditions of the Bible: A Guide to the Bible As It Was at the Start of the Common Era* (Cambridge, MA: Harvard University Press, 1998).

3. George W. E. Nickelsburg and James C. VanderKam, trans., *1 Enoch: A New Translation* (Minneapolis: Fortress Press, 2004), 140.

4. Adapted from the translation of Florentino García Martínez and Eibert J. C. Tigchelaar, *The Dead Sea Scrolls Study Edition* (2 vols., Grand Rapids: Eerdmans, 1997–98), vol. 1, 505.

5. David Winston, trans., *Philo of Alexandria: The Contemplative Life, The Giants, and Selections* (New York: Paulist Press, 1981), 226.

6. Adapted from the translation of Jacob Neusner, *Genesis Rabbah: The Judaic Commentary to the Book of Genesis* (3 vols.; Atlanta: Scholars Press, 1985), vol. 1, 129.

7. James C. VanderKam, trans., *The Book of Jubilees* (2 vols.; Louvain: Peeters, 1989), vol. 2, 6.

8. Ibid., 7.

9. My use of the term "figural" is adapted from Erich Auerbach, "Figura," in Auerbach, *Scenes from the Drama of European Literature* (Minneapolis: University of Minnesota Press, 1984), 11–76. Auerbach tends to restrict this term to typological-apocalyptic interpretation in contrast to the allegorical-Platonic. I am broadening the scope of the term to refer to both symbolic domains, as Auerbach does occasionally (e.g., "Since in figural interpretation one thing stands for another, since one thing represents and signifies the other, figural interpretation is 'allegorical' in the widest sense," p. 54).

10. A striking rabbinic-Platonic figural interpretation occurs on the first page of *Genesis Rabbah*, where the Torah tells how she was created before the universe and then God consulted her as his cosmic blueprint: "He looked at the Torah and created the world." See below, chapter 4, for the analogous scene in Plato's *Timaeus*; and see further Dina Stein, "Rabbinic Interpretation," in *Reading Genesis: Ten Methods*, ed. Ronald Hendel (New York: Cambridge University Press, 2010), 122–23.

CHAPTER 3: Apocalyptic Secrets

1. Sometimes the exilic texts are called "proto-apocalyptic" to distinguish them from the full-blown apocalyptic texts of the Hellenistic period; see generally John J. Collins, *The Apocalyptic Imagination: An Introduction to Jewish Apocalyptic Literature* (2nd ed.; Grand Rapids, MI: Eerdmans, 1998); and Ronald Hendel, "Isaiah and the Transition from Prophecy to Apocalyptic," in *Birkat Shalom: Studies in the Bible, Ancient Near Eastern Literature, and Postbiblical Judaism Presented to Shalom M. Paul*, ed. Chaim Cohen et al. (Winona Lake, IN: Eisenbrauns, 2008), 261–79.

2. Jon D. Levenson, *Sinai and Zion: An Entry into the Jewish Bible* (Minneapolis, MN: Winston Press, 1985), 128. See also Ronald Hendel, "Other Edens," in *Exploring the Longue Durée: Essays in Honor of Lawrence E. Stager*, ed. David Schloen (Winona Lake, IN: Eisenbrauns, 2008), 185–89.

3. Martin McNamara, trans., *Targum Neofiti 1: Genesis* (Collegeville, MN: Michael Glazier, 1992), 215.

4. See *The Oxford Handbook of the Dead Sea Scrolls*, ed. Timothy H. Lim and John J. Collins (Oxford: Oxford University Press, 2010). On the following, see also Crispin H. T. Fletcher-Louis, *All the Glory of Adam: Liturgical Anthropology in the Dead Sea Scrolls* (Leiden: Brill, 2002).

5. Adapted from the translation of Florentino García Martínez and Eibert J. C. Tigchelaar, *The Dead Sea Scrolls Study Edition* (2 vols.; Grand Rapids, MI: Eerdmans, 1997–98), vol. 1, 77–79.

6. Ibid., vol. 1, 555.

7. Ibid., vol. 2, 957.

8. Ibid., vol. 1, 149.

9. Translations of Paul are from the New Revised Standard Version. An excellent edition is *The HarperCollins Study Bible*, ed. Harold W. Attridge (San Francisco: HarperCollins, 2006).

10. See the discussions of this theme in Morna D. Hooker, *From Adam to Christ: Essays on Paul* (Cambridge: Cambridge University Press, 1990); Hooker, *Paul: A Short Introduction* (Oxford: Oneworld, 2003).

11. Martínez and Tigchelaar, trans., *Dead Sea Scrolls*, vol. 2, 1009.

12. Ibid., vol. 1, 75–77.

13. Pesher Habakkuk (1QpHab) vii.4–5; translation adapted from Martínez and Tigchelaar, *Dead Sea Scrolls*, vol. 1, 17.

CHAPTER 4: Platonic Worlds

1. Alfred North Whitehead, *Process and Reality: An Essay on Cosmology* (New York: Free Press, 1978), 39.

2. Adapted from the translation of Robin Waterfield, Plato, *Republic* (Oxford: Oxford University Press, 1993), 244.

3. See Elias Bickerman, *The Jews in the Greek Age* (Cambridge, MA: Harvard University Press, 1988); and Erich S. Gruen, *Heritage and Hellenism: The Reinvention of Jewish Tradition* (Berkeley: University of California Press, 1998).

4. Adapted from the translation of David Winston, *Philo of Alexandria: The Contemplative Life, the Giants, and Selections* (New York: Paulist Press, 1981), 272.

5. See Ronald Hendel, *The Text of Genesis 1–11: Textual Studies and Critical Edition* (New York: Oxford University Press, 1998), 16–20.

6. Harry Wolfson, *Philo: Foundations of Religious Philosophy in Judaism, Christianity, and Islam* (2 vols.; Cambridge, MA: Harvard University Press, 1947).

7. Philo, *Special Laws*. 3.178, trans. Winston, in *Philo of Alexandria*, 79.

8. Winston, *Philo of Alexandria*, 79.

9. See Thomas H. Tobin, *The Creation of Man: Philo and the History of Interpretation* (Washington, DC: Catholic Biblical Association, 1983).

10. Winston, *Philo of Alexandria*, 103.

11. Ibid., 167.

12. Ibid., 173.

13. See Elaine Pagels, *The Gnostic Gospels* (New York: Random House, 1989).

14. Karen L. King, *The Secret Revelation of John* (Cambridge, MA: Harvard University Press, 2006), vii. Citations are to the translation in this edition, occasionally slightly adapted.

15. Peter Brown, *The Body and Society: Men, Women, and Sexual Renunciation in Early Christianity* (New York: Columbia University Press, 1988), 222.

16. John Climacus, *The Ladder of Divine Ascent*, trans. Colm Luibheid and Norman Russell (Mahwah, NJ: Paulist Press, 1982), 74.

17. Brown, *Body and Society*, 294.

18. Quoted in ibid., 222.

19. *The Lives of the Desert Fathers: The Historia Mona-chorum in Aegypto*, trans. Norman Russell (London: Mowbray, 1980), 63.

20. "The Sayings of the Fathers," in *The Desert Fathers*, trans. Helen Waddell (New York: Vintage, 1998), 129.

21. Ibid., 117.

22. Patricia Cox Miller, "Desert Asceticism and 'The Body from Nowhere,'" in *The Poetry of Thought in Late Antiquity: Essays in Imagination and Religion* (Burlington, VT: Ashgate, 2001), 162.

23. Ibid., 159.

24. Ibid., 159.

25. Ibid., 159.

CHAPTER 5: Between the Figure and the Real

1. Dante Alighieri, *The Inferno*, trans. Robert and Jean Hollander (New York: Doubleday, 2000), 171.

2. Quoted in Robert Hollander, *Dante: A Life in Works* (New Haven, CT: Yale University Press, 2001), 98.

3. St. Augustine, *Concerning the City of God against the Pagans*, trans. Henry Bettenson (New York: Penguin Books, 1984), 535.

4. M.-D. Chenu, *Nature, Man, and Society in the Twelfth Century* (Chicago: University of Chicago Press, 1968), 99–145.

5. Ibid., 117; and Peter Harrison, *The Bible, Protestantism,*

and the Rise of Natural Science (Cambridge: Cambridge University Press, 1998), 1.

6. See Amos Funkenstein, *Perceptions of Jewish History* (Berkeley: University of California Press, 1993), 98–121; Moshe Idel, *Absorbing Perfections: Kabbalah and Interpretation* (New Haven: Yale University Press, 2002), 314–51.

7. Ibid., 119–20.

8. Jacques Le Goff, *Medieval Civilization* (Oxford: Basil Blackwell, 1988), 332–33.

9. Quoted in G. R. Evans, *The Language and Logic of the Bible: The Earlier Middle Ages* (Cambridge: Cambridge University Press, 1984), 61.

10. Le Goff, *Medieval Civilization*, 331.

11. Jerome, *Epistle* 64; quoted in Henri de Lubac, *Medieval Exegesis. Vol. I: The Four Senses of Scripture* (Grand Rapids, MI: Eerdmans, 1998), 75.

12. Alan of Lille, *Against the Heretics* 1.30.

13. Alan of Lille, *Rules of Theology*, rule 7; quoted in Gillian Rosemary Evans, *Alan of Lille: The Frontiers of Theology in the Later Twelfth Century* (Cambridge: Cambridge University Press, 1983), 73.

14. Avraham Grossman, "The School of Literal Jewish Exegesis in Northern France," in *Hebrew Bible / Old Testament: The History of Its Interpretation. Vol. I: From the Beginnings to the Middle Ages (Until 1300), Part 2: The Middle Ages*, ed. Magne Sæbø (Göttingen: Vandenhoeck & Ruprecht, 2000), 327–28.

15. Translation adapted from Grossman, "School," 335; see also *Chumash with Rashi's Commentary: Genesis*, trans. A. M. Silbermann (Jerusalem: Feldheim Publishers, 1985), 14.

16. Martin Luther, *Table Talk*, ed. and trans. Theodore G. Tappert (Luther's Works 54; Philadelphia: Fortress Press, 1967), 46 (no. 335).

17. Ibid., 406 (no. 5285), translation revised.

18. Martin Luther, *Career of the Reformer, Vol. II*, trans. George W. Forell (Luther's Works 32; Philadelphia: Fortress Press, 1958), 112 (slightly adapted).

19. Martin Luther, *Lectures on Genesis*, trans. George V. Schick and Paul D. Pahl (8 vols.; Luther's Works 1–8; St. Louis: Concordia Publishing, 1958–66), vol. 1, 184–85. Citations below are to this edition.

20. Quoted in Roland H. Bainton, "The Bible in the Reformation," in *The Cambridge History of the Bible. Vol. 3: The West from the Reformation to the Present Day*, ed. S. L. Greenslade (Cambridge: Cambridge University Press, 1963), 12.

21. Ibid., 21–22.

22. *Selected Writings of Martin Luther*, ed. Theodore G. Tappert (4 vols.; Philadelphia: Fortress Press, 1967), vol. 3, 351.

23. Ibid.

24. Quoted in Roland H. Bainton, "Thomas Muntzer: Revolutionary Firebrand of the Reformation," *The Sixteenth Century Journal* 13 (1982), 9.

25. Luther's response to the radical Reformers also included a broader appeal to reason in the "worldly realm" ("*welltlichem reich*"), for which he cites the role of reason in Genesis when Adam names the animals (Genesis 2:19). Luther writes, "In the secular realm we have to act on the basis of reason (where laws have their origin as well), since God has subjected the temporal powers and the material world to reason (Genesis 2), and he has not sent the Holy Spirit to interfere with it." Niklaus Largier astutely argues that this institutes the modern categorical distinction between the religious and the secular realms; see Largier, "Mysticism, Modernity, and the Invention of Aesthetic Experience," *Representations* 105 (2009), 37–60, quote on p. 42.

26. Mikhail Bakhtin, *Rabelais and His World* (Blooming-ton: Indiana University Press, 1984), 97.

27. M. A. Screech, "Homage to Rabelais," *London Review of Books*, September 20, 1984, 11.

28. Quoted in Lucien Febvre, *The Problem of Unbelief in the Sixteenth Century: The Religion of* Rabelais (Cam-bridge: Harvard University Press 1982), 51.

29. François Rabelais, *Gargantua and Pantagruel*, trans. M. A. Screech (New York: Penguin Books, 2006), 16–17.

30. Quoted in Bainton, "Bible in the Reformation," 15.

31. *Gargantua and Pantagruel*, 18–20.

32. Ibid., 20–21.

33. *Pirqe de Rabbi Eliezer* 23. As a learned Renaissance man, Rabelais probably knew some Hebrew.

34. *Gargantua and Pantagruel*, 21.

35. Ibid., 207.

36. Ibid., 207–8.

37. Ibid., 208.

38. Erich Auerbach, *Mimesis: The Representation of Reality in Western Literature* (Princeton, NJ: Princeton Uni-versity Press, 1953), 281.

39. Luther, *Lectures on Genesis* 2.209.

40. Quoted in Bainton, "Bible in the Reformation," 7.

41. Ibid., 12.

42. Ibid., 12–13.

43. Luther, *Lectures on Genesis* 2.166. Luther, famously, had an appetite for drink; see his comment (*Table Talk*, 207 [no. 3746]): "Tomorrow I have to lecture on the drunkenness of Noah, so I should drink enough this evening to be able to talk about that wickedness as one who knows by experience."

44. Benedict de Spinoza, *Theological-Political Treatise*, trans. Jonathan Israel and Michael Silverthorne (Cam-bridge: Cambridge University Press, 2007), 8.

45. Ibid.

CHAPTER 6: Genesis and Science

1. Martin Luther, *Tischreden* no. 855. See the variant version of the same comment in Martin Luther, *Table Talk*, trans. Theodore G. Tappert (Luther's Works 54; Philadelphia: Fortress Press, 1967), 358–59 (no. 4638), and the comparison of the two in Wilhelm Norlind, "Copernicus and Luther: A Critical Study," *Isis* 44 (1953), 273–76.

2. Wayne Horowitz, *Mesopotamian Cosmic Geography* (Winona Lake, IN: Eisenbrauns, 1998), 4.

3. W. V. Quine, "Two Dogmas of Empiricism," in *Quintessence: Basic Readings from the Philosophy of W. V. Quine*, ed. Roger F. Gibson (Cambridge, MA: Harvard University Press, 2004), 50.

4. Francesca Rochberg, "'The Stars Their Likenesses': Perspectives on the Relation between Celestial Bodies and Gods in Ancient Mesopotamia," in *What is a God? Anthropomorphic and Non-Anthropomorphic Aspects of Deity in Ancient Mesopotamia*, ed. Barbara N. Porter (Winona Lake, IN: Eisenbrauns, 2009), 89.

5. Philo, *On the Preliminary Sciences* 9–11, trans. David Winston, in *Philo of Alexandria: The Contemplative Life, the Giants, and Selections* (New York: Paulist Press, 1981), 213.

6. St. Augustine, *The Literal Meaning of Genesis*, trans. John Hammond Taylor (New York: Newman Press, 1982), vol. 1, 42.

7. Ibid., 48.

8. Ibid., 45.

9. Robert S. Westman, "The Copernicans and the Churches," in *God and Nature: Historical Essays on the Encounter between Christianity and Science*, ed. David C. Lindberg and Ronald L. Numbers (Berkeley: University of California Press, 1986), 81.

10. Maurice A. Finocchiaro, ed. and trans., *The Essential*

Galileo (Indianapolis, IN: Hackett Publishing, 2008), 105.

11. Ibid., 177.

12. Ibid., 292.

13. Ibid., 289.

14. Ibid., 104.

15. Ibid., 115.

16. Ibid., 115–16.

17. Ibid., 116.

18. Ibid., 117.

19. From the *Ratio Studiorum* of 1599; quoted in Rivka Feldhay, *Galileo and the Church: Political Inquisition or Critical Dialogue?* (Cambridge: Cambridge University Press, 1995), 236.

20. Westman, "Copernicans and the Churches," 99.

21. Finocchiaro, *Essential Galileo*, 119.

22. John Paul II, "Faith Can Never Conflict with Reason," *L'Osservatore Romano* [English edition], November 4, 1992, 1–2 (available online at http://www.its.caltech.edu/~nmcenter/sci-cp/sci-9211.html).

23. Jonathan Israel, "Introduction," in Benedict de Spinoza, *Theological-Political Treatise*, trans. Michael Silverthorne and Jonathan Israel (Cambridge: Cambridge University Press, 2007), viii.

24. Ibid., 97–98.

25. Ibid., 98.

26. Finocchiaro, *Essential Galileo*, 183.

27. Spinoza, *Theological-Political Treatise*, 98.

28. Ibid., 92.

29. Ibid., 100.

30. *Ibn Ezra's Commentary on the Pentateuch: Genesis*, trans. H. Norman Strickman and Arthur M. Silver (New York: Menorah Publishing, 1988), 151.

31. Spinoza, *Treatise*, 120.

32. Ibid., 122.

33. Ibid., 130.

34. Ibid., 132.

35. Ibid., 188.

36. Ibid., 194.

37. Quoted in Paul Hazard, *The European Mind: 1680–1715* (Cleveland, OH: Meridian Books, 1963), 184.

38. See Don Cameron Allen, *The Legend of Noah: Renaissance Rationalism in Art, Science, and Letters* (Urbana: University of Illinois Press, 1949), 113–37; Anthony Grafton, *New Worlds, Ancient Texts: The Power of Tradition and the Shock of Discovery* (Cambridge, MA: Harvard University Press, 1992).

39. Walter Raleigh, *The History of the World: Book I* (Oxford: Oxford University Press, 1829 [1614]), 334.

40. Quoted in Grafton, *New Worlds*, 211.

41. Quoted in Zvi Ben-Dor Benite, *The Ten Lost Tribes: A World History* (New York: Oxford University Press, 2009), 142.

42. *The Bible According to Mark Twain*, ed. Howard G. Baetzhold and Joseph B. McCullough (New York: Simon and Schuster, 1996), 316.

43. Quoted in Paolo Rossi, *The Dark Abyss of Time: The History of the Earth and the History of Nations from Hooke to Vico* (Chicago: University of Chicago Press, 1987), 116.

44. Robert Bakewell, *An Introduction to Geology* (London: J. Harding, 1813), 19.

45. Augustine, *Literal Meaning of Genesis*, vol. 1, 132–38.

46. Rossi, *Dark Abyss of Time*, ix.

47. Quoted in Stephen Jay Gould, *The Richness of Life: The Essential Stephen Jay Gould*, ed. Steven Rose (New York: Norton, 2007), 550.

48. Ibid., 550–51.

49. Charles Wycliffe Goodwin, "Mosaic Cosmology," in *Essays and Reviews: The 1860 Text and Its Reading*,

ed. Victor Shea and William Whitla (Charlottesville: University Press of Virginia, 2000), 370.

50. Henry Bristow Wilson, "Séances Historique de Genève: The National Church," in *Essays and Reviews*, 306.

51. Johann Gottfried Herder, *Against Pure Reason: Writings on Religion, Language, and History*, ed. and trans. Marcia Bunge (Minneapolis, MN: Fortress Press, 1992), 259. On Herder's (and his contemporaries') reconstitution of biblical authority on cultural rather than theological grounds, see Jonathan Sheehan, *The Enlightenment Bible: Translation, Scholarship, Culture* (Princeton: Princeton University Press, 2005).

52. Samuel Wilberforce, review of *Essays and Reviews*, *The Quarterly Review* 109 (1861), 288.

53. Søren Kierkegaard, *Concluding Unscientific Postscript*, trans. Alastair Hannay (Cambridge: Cambridge University Press, 2009; original publication 1846).

54. "Satires by Lewis Carroll and Others," in *Essays and Reviews*, 818.

55. Quoted in David O. Beale, *In Pursuit of Purity: American Fundamentalism Since 1850* (Greenville, SC: Unusual Publications, 1986), 375.

56. Ibid., 375–76.

57. A. A. Hodge and Benjamin B. Warfield, "Inspiration," *Presbyterian Review* 2 (1881), 238.

58. Ibid., 242.

59. Kern Robert Trembath, *Evangelical Theories of Biblical Inspiration: A Review and Proposal* (New York: Oxford University Press, 1987), 26.

60. Hodge and Warfield, "Inspiration," 239.

61. Charles A. Briggs, *Whither? A Theological Question for the Times* (New York: Scribner's, 1889), 72–73.

62. Ibid., 21.

63. See Ernest R. Sandeen, *The Roots of Fundamentalism:*

British and American Millenarianism, 1800–1930 (Chicago: University of Chicago Press, 1970), ch. 8 ("The Fundamentals").

64. J. J. Reeve, "My Personal Experience with the Higher Criticism," in *The Fundamentals: A Testimony to the Truth*, ed. A. C. Dixon and Reuben A. Torrey (12 vols.; Chicago: Testimony Publishing, 1910–15), vol. 3, 98–99.

65. Ibid., 114.

66. Ibid., 111.

67. Frédéric Bettex, "The Bible and Modern Criticism," *Fundamentals*, vol. 4, 89–90.

68. Quoted in George M. Marsden, *Understanding Fundamentalism and Evangelicalism* (Grand Rapids, MI: Eerdmans Publishing, 1991), 1.

69. Ibid., 119.

70. Ibid., 121.

CHAPTER 7: Modern Times

1. Mark A. Noll, The *Civil War as a Theological Crisis* (Chapel Hill: University of North Carolina Press, 2006).

2. Stephen R. Haynes, *Noah's Curse: The Biblical Justification of American Slavery* (New York: Oxford University Press, 2002).

3. Quoted in David Brion Davis, *Inhuman Bondage: The Rise and Fall of Slavery in the New World* (New York: Oxford University Press, 2006), 66.

4. Ibid.

5. On Lincoln's biblical eloquence, see Robert Alter, *Pen of Iron: American Prose and the King James Bible* (Princeton: Princeton University Press, 2010), 11–19.

6. Including Paul's command that slaves be obedient to their masters (Ephesians 6:5; Colossians 3:22; and 1 Timothy 6:1); see Allen D. Callahan, *The Talking Book:*

African Americans and the Bible (New Haven: Yale University Press, 2006), 30–38.

7. Noll, *Civil War*, 160–61.

8. Quoted in Noll, *Civil War*, 31–32.

9. Ibid., 205.

10. Elizabeth Cady Stanton, ed., *The Woman's Bible. Part I: Comments on Genesis, Exodus, Leviticus, Numbers and Deuteronomy* (New York: European Publishing, 1895), 10, 31.

11. Ibid., 21.

12. For a recent overview, see Ronald Hendel, Chana Kronfeld, and Ilana Pardes, "Gender and Sexuality," in *Reading Genesis: Ten Methods*, ed. R. Hendel (Cambridge: Cambridge University Press, 2010), 71–91.

13. *The Poems of Emily Dickinson: Reading Edition*, ed. R. W. Franklin (Cambridge, MA: Harvard University Press, 1999), no. 1263. Citations are to the numeration of this edition.

14. Ibid.

15. Quoted in Jane Donahue Eberwein, *Dickinson: Strategies of Limitation* (Amherst: University of Massachusetts Press, 1985), 78.

16. Theodore Parker, *Theodore Parker's Experience as a Minister, with Some Account of His Early Life, and Education for the Ministry* (Boston: Rufus Leighton, 1859), 38–40.

17. *Poems of Emily Dickinson*, nos. 1438, 1415.

18. Ibid., no. 503.

19. Quoted in James McIntosh, *Nimble Believing: Dickinson and the Unknown* (Ann Arbor: University of Michigan Press, 2000), 89.

20. Ibid.

21. Ibid., 84.

22. *Poems of Emily Dickinson*, no. 1577.

23. McIntosh, *Nimble Believing*, 67.

24. *Poems of Emily Dickinson*, no. 1734.

25. *Ibid.*, no. 1411.

26. Quoted in Louis Begley, *The Tremendous World I Have Inside My Head: Franz Kafka: A Biographical Essay* (New York: Atlas, 2008), 93.

27. Adapted from Malcolm Pasley's translation in Franz Kafka, *The Great Wall of China and Other Short Works* (London: Penguin Books, 1991), 161.

28. Quoted in Robert Alter, *Necessary Angels: Tradition and Modernity in Kafka, Benjamin, and Scholem* (Cambridge, MA: Harvard University Press, 1991), 19.

29. Max Brod, *Franz Kafka: A Biography* (2nd ed.; New York: Schocken, 1960), 180.

30. Primo Levi, "Note to Franz Kafka's *The Trial*," in Levi, *The Black Hole of Auschwitz*, ed. Marco Belpoliti (Malden, MA: Polity Press, 2005), 140.

31. Breon Mitchell, "Translator's Preface," in Franz Kafka, *The Trial*, trans. Mitchell (New York: Schocken Books, 1998), xix. Citations are to this translation.

32. Kafka, *Trial*, 10 (translation adapted).

33. Roberto Calasso, *K* (New York: Alfred Knopf, 2005), 293.

34. Ritchie Robertson, *Kafka: Judaism, Politics, and Literature* (Oxford: Clarendon Press, 1985), 104.

35. Kafka, *Trial*, 9.

36. Ibid., 12.

37. Ibid., 136.

38. Ibid., 29.

39. Brod, *Kafka: A Biography*, 178.

40. In the following I follow the numeration and adapt the translations of Malcolm Pasley, "The Complete Aphorisms," in *Great Wall*, 79–98. See also the translation by Michael Hofmann, *The Zürau Aphorisms of Franz Kafka*, ed. Roberto Calasso (New York: Schocken, 2006).

41. Alter, *Necessary Angels*, 74; see further idem, *Canon and Creativity: Modern Writing and the Authority of Scripture* (New Haven: Yale University Press, 2000), 63–96.

42. "Complete Aphorisms," no. 18.

43. Quoted in Calasso, *K*, 301; cf. aphorism 69.

44. "Complete Aphorisms," no. 84.

45. See Ronald Hendel, "Other Edens," in *Exploring the Longue Durée: Essays in Honor of Lawrence E. Stager*, ed. David Schloen (Winona Lake, IN: Eisenbrauns, 2008), 185–89.

46. "Complete Aphorisms," no. 64/65.

47. Ibid., no. 106.

48. Ibid., no. 86.

49. "On Parables," in *Great Wall*, 184.

50. This is a complication of the romantic idea of fiction as creative illumination (see M. H. Abrams, *The Mirror and the Lamp: Romantic Theory and the Critical Tradition* [Oxford: Oxford University Press, 1953]), but for Kafka the light can hardly penetrate the real world, or may be merely a rumor.

51. Erich Auerbach, *Mimesis: The Representation of Reality in Western Literature*, trans. Willard R. Trask (Princeton: Princeton University Press, 1953), 557.

52. On Auerbach's life and work, see Geoffrey Green: *Literary Criticism and the Structures of History: Erich Auerbach and Leo Spitzer* (Lincoln: University of Nebraska Press, 1982).

53. Robert Alter, "Literature," in *Reading Genesis: Ten Methods*, ed. Ronald Hendel (Cambridge: Cambridge University Press, 2010), 16.

54. Auerbach, *Mimesis*, 23.

55. Ibid., 13.

56. Ibid., 8.

57. Ibid., 8.

58. Ibid., 9–10.

59. Ibid., 12.

60. Ibid., 11.

61. Ibid., 23.

62. Ibid., 23.

63. Ibid., 15.

64. Ibid., 15–16.

AFTERWORD: Stories of Our Alley

1. The novel was initially serialized in a Cairo newspaper in 1959 and was published as a book in Lebanon in 1967; see Richard Jacquemond, *Conscience of the Nation: Writers, State, and Society in Modern Egypt* (Cairo: American University in Cairo Press, 2008), 1–5, 56–61, 227–29.

2. Naguib Mahfouz, *Children of the Alley*, trans. Peter Theroux (New York: Doubleday, 1996), 38.

3. Ibid., 373.

4. Quoted in Sasson Somekh, *The Changing Rhythm: A Study of Najīb Mahfūz's Novels* (Leiden: Brill, 1973), 142.

INDEX OF CITATIONS

GENERAL INDEX

Abraham: call of as spiritual quest, 94; and offering of Isaac, 232–238; walking with God, 50

accommodation of Scripture to human intellects, 161–162

accommodation of Scripture to science: ended in nineteenth century, 182, 195; seen as unnecessary, 175–176

Adam: curse on, 201–202; Kafka's Josef K as, 221; naming of animals, 257n25; twofold creation of, in Philo, 92–93

Adam, glory of: in apocalypticism, 70–75, 105; becomes Christ's glory in New Testament, 76–77; and Desert Fathers, 104

Adam, Last, 75–79

Adam and Eve, 39–44; Luther's criticism of Platonic interpretation, 122; in nineteenth century biblical scholarship, 184–185. *See also* Eve

African peoples, justification for enslavement of, 197–204

"afterlife" of a text as transformation, 4

Against the Robbing and Murdering Hordes of Peasants (Luther), 127–128

Alan of Lille, 115

allegorical interpretation: Augustine on, 111–112; Luther's criticism of, 123–124; by Paul, 96–97; in Philo, 55–56, 91–92; Rabelais's criticism of, 134–135. *See also* figural interpretations

Allegorical Interpretation (Philo), 55–56

ambiguity in J, 23, 41, 43

angels in Qumran community, 71–72

antiquity of the earth and chronology of Genesis, 179

apocalyptic communities. *See* Essenes (Qumran community)

apocalyptic dualism, 79–82. *See also* dual reality

apocalyptic expectations as anachronism, 4

apocalypticism: concept of reality in, 9; as part of history, according to Luther, 69, 139; in Rashi, 118–119; refashioning of Genesis in, 67; as response to crisis, 64

apples: as aphrodisiacs in Middle Ages, 2; hidden meanings in Middle Ages, 113–114; in Kafka, 218, 221

Arias Montano, Benito, 177

asceticism: of Desert Fathers, 103–104; as foretastes of life in Garden of Eden, 71–72

astronomy, ancient Near Eastern, 147, 159

atheist response to Genesis, 1

Auerbach, Erich, 229–241; narrative style gives rise to interpretation, 5; on realism in Rabelais, 136; relationship between realism and figuralism, 9

Augustine of Hippo: on chronology of Genesis, 180; and Galileo, 161–162; on Garden of Eden, 111–112; harmonizing *Timaeus* with Genesis, 180; hierarchy of knowledge, 155; on multiple truths in Scripture, 110; and nature, 112–113

authority of interpretations: in Church Fathers, 114; and Galileo, 160–161, 164; rise of science as challenge to, 146

authority of Scripture: undermined by critical consciousness, 240–241

Babylonian Creation story, 30–32

Babylonian Exile, apocalypticism as response to, 64

Babylonian Exile, return from, 60. *See also* postexilic period

Babylonian Flood story, 26–29

Bakewell, Robert, 179

Beersheba and inconsistencies in text, 48

Ben Israel, Manasseh, 177

Bethel and inconsistencies in text, 48

Bettex, Frédéric, 193–194

Bible as corrupted text, 188–191

birds, sending out: Luther's figural use of, 138–139; variation in Flood stories, 26–29

body: denigration of in gnosticism, 103; role of in Desert Fathers, 106–109; role of in Platonic life practices, 102–103; transformation into immortal body, 76

Book of Mormon, 178

Briggs, Charles, 191–192

Bruno, Giordano, 177

Cain, inconsistencies in text, 47–48

Cain's wife, inconsistencies in text, 48

Canaan (Noah's grandson) as justification for slavery, 198–200

Canaanites, historical context of, 173

divine agency omitted from natural selection, 183

divine craftsman in Plato, 87

divine names in J and P sources, 20

divine origin of Scripture, 58–60, 142–144, 171

documentary hypothesis, 174. *See also* E source (Elohist source); J source (Yahwist source); P source

dragons transformed into natural order of cosmos, 38

dual reality: in Desert Fathers, 106; of material world and ideal world in Plato, 9, 84–88; this world as flawed version of more perfect world, 11. *See also* apocalyptic dualism; Platonic duality

early modern times (1200-1600): figural interpretation yields to more realistic sense, 10, 110; return to single world, 11

Ecclesiastes, 21

eighteenth century: Genesis viewed as myth or legend, 182; questioning divine origin of scripture, 143–144. *See also* science, rise of

Einstein, Albert, 175

Elijah, 50

Elohist source (E). *See* E source (Elohist source)

emotions: of God in P, 21–22; of Yahweh in J, 20–21, 23

end of days: in apocalypticism,

67–70; as hidden world in Genesis, 11

end of time and primal light, 119

Enlightenment. *See* eighteenth century

Enoch, book of, 50–51, 61

eroticism in Garden of Eden: in Dickinson, 213; Eve as erotic temptress, 5. *See also* sex in paradise

errors: and interpretation of corrupted copies, 191; role of in life, 6–8

E source (Elohist source): Abraham and Isaac, 234; definition, 17; representational style in, 238

Essays and Reviews, 184–185

Essenes (Qumran community), 70–75; attitude toward body, 104–105; saw world under the authority of evil powers, 80; as site of river of paradise, 71–72. *See also* Dead Sea Scrolls

Eve: in Dickinson, 210; as erotic temptress, 5; as justification for subjection of women, 204–207; as "luminous Thought" in gnosticism, 100, 101; Luther on creation of from Adam's rib, 126. *See also* Adam and Eve

evil creator in gnosticism, 98

Ezekiel, Book of, 29–30, 66–67

Ezra the priest as interpreter of Torah, 46

Falwell, Jerry, 194

fictions, Genesis as: in Dickinson, 209–211; in Kafka, 215–216, 224–225, 228; and modern realism, 240; romantic idea of, 265n50; as starting point of Western literature, 230; usefulness of, 244

figs as aphrodisiacs in Middle Ages, 2

figural interpretations, 45–62; and apocalyptic and Platonic philosophy, 9; and conflict of science and plain sense, 155–156; day-age theory and gap theory as, 179–180; decline of in Renaissance, 137–138; definition, 249n5, 252n9; dominant before Renaissance, 10, 61; and Galileo's harmonization of science and scripture, 160–161; in *Genesis Rabbah*, 252n10; mocked by Rabelais, 136–137; in Rashi, 118–119; yielding to realistic sense by early modern period, 110. *See also* allegorical interpretation

figural interpretations of nature, 163–164, 181

Flood story: antecedents in Near Eastern myth, 26–32; cause of in *Gilgamesh*, 28–29; edited from J and P sources, 18–24; survival of Hurtaly in Flood (parody), 132–133

forms, Platonic, 86, 93

freedom of speech and religion

and methods of biblical interpretation, 168, 175

fruitful misunderstanding, 7–8

fundamentalism, rise of, 186–195

Fundamentals: A Testimony to the Truth, 192

Galileo, 157–166; criticized Genesis as unscientific, 6; and historical-critical method of criticism, 172; outdated theology of, 164–165

gap theory, 179–180, 181

Garden of Eden: in apocalyptic religion, 9; Augustine on, 111–112; in Dickinson, 212–215; in gnosticism, 100; from J source, 39–44; in Kafka, 216–219, 223–225, 226; and later interpretations of, 5; in Luther, 125, 127–128; in Middle Ages asceticism, 2; Paul's vision of, 75–79; in Rashi, 117; roots in ancient Near Eastern traditions, 28–29; wordplay in, 20. *See also* paradise; rivers of paradise

Gargantua and Pantagruel (Rabelais), 129–137

Garrison, William Lloyd, 204

gender relationships: and biblical justification for women's rights, 207; in J source, 42; in P source, 38

genealogies: and discoveries in New World, 178; Genesis as, 17; irrelevance to Luther, 140; irrelevance to Rashi, 140;

and New World discoveries, 176–177; parody of by Rabelais, 131–132, 140

Genesis: as complex literary work, 233–234; as cryptic version of more perfect text, 11, 49–54, 139–141; as divine revelation, 49, 58–60, 142–144; as literature, 231–232; as magical realism, 12; as myths and legends, 182, 250n10; in nineteenth century biblical scholarship, 185; oldest poetry in, 15–17; as perfect, 56–58, 141; as relevant, 53–56, 139–141

Genesis Rabbah, 57–58, 116, 252n10

geological time and chronology of Genesis, 179

giants in Genesis, 130

Gihon river and Jerusalem, 65–67

Gilgamesh, 26–29

glory. *See* Adam, glory of; Christ, glory of, and Paul's apocalyptic knowledge

gnosticism, 98–102, 103

God: as agent of Creation, 147; compassionate in J, 43; distinctions in character between J and P sources, 19; as luminous and perfect in gnosticism, 99; rise of science as challenge to, 146; transcendent in P, 21–22, 23

good and evil in apocalypticism,

81–82. *See also* tree of knowledge of good and evil

good as goal of Platonic philosophy, 86

Goodwin, Charles, 184

Greco-Roman age: harmonizing Genesis with Platonic cosmology, 153; rise of apocalyptic expectations, 64

Greek ways of thought: criticized by Spinoza, 142–143; influence on Judaism, 84. *See also* Platonism

Grimké, Sarah, 205–206

Hagar, inconsistencies in text, 48

Hagar and Sarah, allegorical interpretation of by Paul, 96–97

Ham (Noah's son), 199

harmonization of Genesis and science, in nineteenth century, 182, 195

harmony and structure. *See* order and structure

heaven as Platonic world of pure forms, 95

heavenly bodies, creation of in P, 35

heliocentric model of universe, 146, 158, 163–164

"helper corresponding to him," in Rashi, 118

Herder, J. G., 185, 230

hidden meanings: Abraham's call, in Philo, 94, 103; Adam's twofold creation, in Philo, 92–93; in apocalypticism,

original meanings *vs.* interpretation, 3

Original Sin: as interpretation of Garden of Eden, 5; in Kafka, 218

Osiander, Andreas, 157

Palestinian Targums, 69

Palladius, 107

Pambo, Abba, 105–106

parables of Kafka, 222–229

paradise: Christ's glory transforming the world, 78–79; evil forces will be transformed, 80–81; Jerusalem Temple as, 65–66. *See also* Garden of Eden

Parker, Theodore, 208–209

parodies of the Bible, 129–137

patriarchal hierarchy and Eve's desire for forbidden fruit, 42

patriarchs, importance of, 17

Paul, Apostle: apocalypticism in, 75–79; on slavery, 263n6; vision of heavenly mysteries and Platonic philosophy, 96; world as under the authority of evil powers, 80

peasants' rebellion and apocalypticism, 127–128

Penn, William, 178

perfection as attribute of Torah, 56–58, 141

Philo of Alexandria: and Abraham's call, 94, 103; allegorical interpretation in, 55–56, 91–92; harmonizing Genesis with Platonic cosmology, 153;

reading the Bible through the lens of Greek philosophy, 90–95; on Septuagint, 89

philosophy as queen of the sciences, 153–154

plain senses of Genesis: and conflict with scientific knowledge, 155; and doctrine of inerrancy of scripture, 187–188; genuine sense not necessarily true, 171; *vs.* interpretation, 4; in Rashi's interpretations, 116, 120; readable as realistic, 11; still available, 5

planets as gods in ancient astronomy, 147–149

Platonic duality: anachronistic when applied to Genesis, 4; buried with rise of Galilean science, 163; concept of reality in, 9; influence on translators of Septuagint, 89; Luther's criticism of, 123. *See also* dual reality

Platonism: harmonization of *Timaeus* with Genesis 1, 89–90, 180; Kafkaesque revision of, 225

poetry, old, 15–17

popular culture references to Genesis, 1

postexilic period: development of concept of End of Days, 68–69; development of concept of messiah, 51–53; development of new ways of living according to apocalyptic

postexilic period (*cont.*)
secrets, 70. *See also* Babylonian Exile, return from
precious stones motif, 30
Priestly source (P), 17
Principia Mathematica (Newton), 166–167
problematic features in style of Genesis, 10
prophecy: in apocalypticism, 53, 69, 139; in Blessing of Jacob, 15–16. *See also* Judah, prophecy about
Protestant Reformation: based on alliance between reason and plain sense, 122; and decline of cryptic interpretation, 139. *See also* Luther, Martin
P source: Creation story of, 32–39; emotions of God, 21–22; flood in, 19, 22, 23
psychological perspective in Genesis, 10
Pythagorean school, 86

Qumran community. *See* Essenes (Qumran community)

Rabelais, François, 129–137, 140
Raleigh, Walter, 177
Rashi, 115–120; criticized figural interpretations, 6; explanations of Scripture, 138; on genealogies, 140
realism: and Galileo, 163; leading away from religious horizons, 240; modern return to, 12; in Rabelais, 134; style of Genesis *vs.* Homer, 10, 238
reality: changing meaning of and rise of science, 146; Genesis as key to understanding of, 3, 8–13; Genesis's influence on representation of, 231–232, 239; in J source is harsh and unforgiving, 41; multifaceted picture in combination of J and P, 24; as ordered structure in P, 23, 38–39; in poetry of Emily Dickinson, 208; in Western civilization, 230. *See also* dual reality
reason: attacks on by fundamentalists, 193; *vs.* inspiration by Holy Spirit, 170, 173; as only authority for interpretation, 115, 143; reconciling conflict with historical facts, 126, 257n25
Reeve, J. J., 192–193
relevance as assumption about Scripture, 53–56, 139–141
Renaissance: figural interpretation becomes problematic, 10; questioning of assumptions about Genesis, 137–138
repetitions: as evidence of hidden meanings, 57–58; as framing device, 34; and narrative in Abraham and Isaac, 236–237
Republic (Plato), 84–85, 86,

102. *See also* cave, allegory of (Plato)

retelling of biblical stories in Mahfouz, 242–245

ritual practices and access to other realities, 61

rivers of paradise: in apocalypticism, 65–67; in Dead Sea Scroll group belief, 71; location of, 54–55

romantic sensibility regarding the Bible, 185, 265n50

sacred writing and development of apocalypticism, 64

Sarah and Hagar as figures of hierarchy of learning, 153–154

Sayings of the Fathers, 105–106

science, rise of: becomes professionalized, 166; and challenge to nature of God, authority, and reality, 146; figural interpretation becomes problematic, 10

science and theology independent of each other, 175–176

scientific method applied to Bible, 167–169, 170–171

"Scripture alone" *(sola scriptura)* principle, 121, 172

sea creatures, creation of, and birth of new life in Dead Sea, 66–67

Secret Revelation of John, 98–102

self-consciousness in J, 41

Septuagint, origin of, 88–89

seventeenth and eighteenth

century questions on divine origin of Scripture, 143–144

sex in paradise, 71–72. *See also* eroticism in Garden of Eden

sexual awareness in J, 41

Sforno, Obadiah, 139

Shiloh as secret name of messiah, 53

Simon, Richard, 175–176

sixteenth and seventeenth century debate on biblical connection with New World, 176–177

sky in ancient cosmology, 147–148

slavery in the United States as theological problem, 197–204

snake as Satan, 5

sola scriptura ("Scripture alone") principle, 121, 172

soul, ascent of, in Philo, 89–95

spatial domains, creation of, 35–37

Spinoza, Baruch: criticized Genesis as unscientific, 6; inconsistencies and puzzles in the text, 173–174; inventor of procedures of modern biblical scholarship, 167–168; questioned divine origin of Scripture, 142–144, 171

Stanton, Elizabeth Cady, 206–207

Starry Messenger (Galileo), 157

Steno, Nicolas, 179

stories, retelling, 245

structure. *See* order and structure

symbolism: authority for, 114–120; buried with rise of Galilean science, 163; in Middle Ages, 113–114

Ten Lost Tribes of Israel, 177, 178
Theological-Political Treatise (Spinoza), 142–144, 167–168, 175
theology, primacy of in Middle Ages, 154
Theory of the Earth (Hutton), 179
Timaeus (Plato), 86–87, 89–90, 180
time and temporal order of the cosmos, 35
time periods when dualistic forces rule, 81–82
Tower of Babel, in Kafka, 222–224
translation: Luther's translation of Bible into German, 127; Platonic influence on translators of Septuagint, 89–90
tree of knowledge of good and evil: and future paradise as new Garden of Eden, 66–67; in gnosticism, 100; in J source, 41; in Kafka, 218–220, 226–227
Trial (Kafka), 215–229
tribal blessings and curses, 15, 33
tribal cultures, 16–17
truth: in Abraham and Isaac, 237–238; capacity for in poetry, 215; in debate over slavery, 205; hunger for in

fundamentalism, 194; in Kafka, 228
truth and error, relationship between, 3
twelfth century Renaissance and shift in interpretation, 115

U.S. Civil War and public policy based on scripture, 203
Ussher, James, 179
Utnapishtim (Babylonian Noah), 26–29

"vault of heaven" in ancient astronomy, 149
visible and invisible things in Platonic thought, 84

Warfield, Benjamin B., 188–189
way of life: in apocalyptic communities, 70; Plato's philosophy as, 102
Western civilization: engagement with Genesis, 2–3; Genesis as document of, 239; threat to, 229; values of, 230
Western hemisphere. *See* New World (Western hemisphere), discovery of
Western literature and two styles of realism, 10
Whither? (Briggs), 191–192
Wilberforce, Samuel, 183, 185–186
Wilson, Henry, 184
woman suffrage movement, 205–207
women, 204–207

Women's Bible (Stanton),
206–207
wordplay: in Flood story, 20, 22;
between "man" and "soil" in J
source, 40; and search for hidden meaning, 58
worldviews: of apocalypticism,
81; conflict between faith and
reason, 193; modern readers

outside of history, 240–241;
of translators of Septuagint,
89
World War I and Kafka, 215

Yahwist source (J). *See* J source
(Yahwist source)
Yaldabaoth (Child of Chaos) in
gnosticism, 98–99